september
LETTERS

Brittany Snow + Jaspre Guest

HARPER
DESIGN
An Imprint of HarperCollinsPublishers

HarperCollins books may be purchased for educational, business, or sales promotional use. For information please email the Special Markets Department at SPsales@harpercollins.com.

Published in 2023 by
Harper Design
An Imprint of HarperCollins *Publishers*
195 Broadway
New York, NY 10007
Tel: (212) 207-7000
Fax: (855) 746-6023
harperdesign@harpercollins.com
www.hc.com

Distributed throughout the world by
HarperCollins *Publishers*
195 Broadway
New York, NY 10007

SEPTEMBER LETTERS is a registered trademark of September Letters LLC

Cover design by Alexa Sparacio
Book design by Raphael Geroni and Lynne Yeamans

Photography and illustration credits:
Back cover photo and pages 2, 10 (portraits of Brittany Snow and Jaspre Guest): Alec Kugler; Pages 16, 24, 28, 36, 42, 46, 48, 56, 69, 71, 74, 81, 84, 92, 94, 98, 101, 112, 116, 128, 131, 134 (lifestyle imagery): Lauren Withrow; Page 5 (illustration): Rachel Joanis; Page 6 (quill): courtesy of September Letters; Page 7 (paper airplane): courtesy of September Letters; Pages 6, 7, 16, 21, 36, 56, 69, 74, 81, 94, 101, 116, 122 (sitcky notes): Shutterstock/FOTO Eak; Pages 8, 9, 138, 139 (paper): Shutterstock/Stephen Rees; Pages 12, 48 (sticky note): Shutterstock/Anna L-G; Back cover and pages 12, 18, 19, 20, 21, 22, 25, 35, 43, 46, 47, 54, 55, 59, 61, 64, 65, 67, 68, 69, 72, 73, 79, 93, 96, 99, 102, 110, 115, 123 (tape): Shutterstock/Valery Evlakhov; Back cover and pages 12, 19, 20, 22, 35, 47, 54, 55, 59, 61, 64, 65, 69, 71, 73, 79, 93, 96, 99, 102, 110, 115, 123 (paper): Shutterstock/Pakhnyushchy; Back cover and pages 13, 24, 46, 50, 67, 98, 120, 129 (notes): Shutterstock/PixMarket; Page 18 (typewriter): photo courtesy of Tom Hanks; Pages 21, 25, 43, 68, 72, 137 (paper): Shutterstock/Nenov Brothers Images; Pages 32, 53, 109 (card): Shutterstock/SCOTTCHAN; Page 33, 91 (card): Shutterstock/LiliGraphie; Pages 40, 48, 112 (stickie note): Shutterstock/Daniel Kite; Page 79 (book): photo courtesy of Horacio Salinas

ISBN 978-0-06-324222-7
Library of Congress Control Number: 2022947545

Printed in Thailand

First Printing, 2023

Dedicated to Billie and Papaya

Contents

___

Introduction — 11

1
JOY
+
HAPPINESS

— 17 —

2
RESILIENCE
+
HEALING

— 37 —

3
COURAGE
+
STRENGTH

— 57 —

4

LOVE
+
LOSS

— 75 —

5

FEAR
+
ANXIETY

— 95 —

6

FRIENDSHIP
+
COMMUNITY

— 117 —

Resources — 140

Acknowledgments — 142

TO WRITE A LETTER IS TO...

Share your heart.

INVITE OTHERS IN.

Start a conversation.

FEEL AT HOME.

Give hope.

RECEIVE.

TRY.

Listen.

OFFER.

Heal.

BE.

Know.

TO WRITE A LETTER IS
TO KNOW YOU'RE NOT
ALONE.

Introduction

Like all good stories, ours began with a rooftop pool party in New York City. A party neither of us wanted to go to but dutifully attended. Introverted extroverted wallflowers, we found our way under a cabana, chatting like long-lost sisters sharing an instant connection. The type of connection that you can pick up right where you left off, even when it is right at the beginning. In between our duties at the party, where Britt was hosting and Jaspre was running the press and guest list, we shared a common bond. Long after the party ended, we would always pick up where we left off.

As our friendship formed that night, our lives shifted. We grew closer and closer despite living in different cities. Hour-long conversations felt like two minutes. Dinners, seconds. Our conversations covered a huge range of topics, but we wanted to do something—really do something—that helped people.

Years later, in 2019, we found ourselves living in New York City at the same time. One night, we met up at a local bar. As we sat there, we felt the time was right to put our efforts together with a plan. From Britt's story, September Letters was born.

When I was a teenager, I read an article in a fitness magazine about the writer's struggle to recover from depression, anxiety, and an eating disorder. In her story I saw myself. Somehow, her words were ones I had not yet spoken out loud or had any understanding of. Suddenly, I didn't feel so alone. There was someone else who had recovered from what I was going through. There was hope and it was right in front of me in someone else's story. I tore the article from the magazine, folded it, and put it in my back pocket. It served as a reminder that I, too, could get better.

Years later, I shared my story of battling depression and anxiety in a magazine. I recalled finding that article when I was a teenager and how it helped me realize I wasn't alone. Shortly after my article came out, I was at a coffee shop when a young girl came up to me, eyes brimming with tears. The girl reached into her back pocket and pulled out my article. I realized then how our stories are always connected.

The beginning of my mental health journey started in September and the month has always signified the choice of choosing myself. To choose a way out of the darkness. September, to me, is a reminder that we can always choose to start again, connect to others, and find the hope we are looking for.

Dear September

Britt continued to tell Jaspre how that moment connected to one of her longtime dreams: She'd always wanted to launch a project that combined her love of letter-writing and her mental health advocacy. Letter-writing, and writing in general, is one of the purest forms of sharing a story. There's a transcendence and power to putting your vulnerability on the page. Writing is a true form of self-care, Britt believes, as it requires you to take the time to be present with your emotions. It allows you to share your most raw truths with someone else—inspiring them in turn to do the same.

By writing and sharing our stories, we see that we are not alone. This happened for Britt. And it happened for the girl who saw Britt in the coffee shop.

> BY WRITING AND SHARING OUR STORIES, WE SEE THAT WE ARE NOT ALONE.

Jaspre was used to taking ideas and making them a reality. She saw that people needed to feel less alone and more connected. For her entire life, Jaspre has been involved in charitable work. This drive to help people was one of the first things that ignited her and Britt's friendship. They had finally found the tool that they were looking for, and it was the idea of helping people through letter-writing.

So began our real partnership in something greater than ourselves and our stories. Over countless breakfasts and coffees, and in between client meetings and fittings and on planes and film sets, we made notes and sketched our ideas. We were building a platform for people to share their stories—their authentic, unedited, true, real stories. It was through all of this connection and truth-telling that September Letters was born.

What began as a secret project that no one knew about other than our dogs (Billie and Papaya, patiently waiting under the table at every early meeting—now Charlie and Quince do the same) has blossomed into a community with thousands of members worldwide. September Letters is a place of connection and truth. There is no judgment. Only the understanding that we are all struggling with something and need to feel seen.

Today, more than ever, we need to safeguard our mental health. Letter-writing, in its various forms, is a beautiful, cathartic way to do just that. Just putting your thoughts on paper (or the screen, or a Post-it Note, or in a journal) is a transformational act. When we write, we share. And when we share, we crack open new portals—and heal.

That is what September Letters is all about. Writing a letter, even if you never plan to share it with anyone, is a vulnerable and courageous act on its own. It's a way to say to yourself or to someone: I see you. I'm here. I feel that, too. You're not alone.

We are growing as a society. Little by little we are starting to fully see how much we need to move through this time and space as a collective unit. If we form a community of openness, we may gain strength in our similarities. We have always found recovery in knowing we aren't alone—and we want to share that with others.

We are so proud and in awe of how the September Letters community has grown. We are also proud of our partnership with The Mental Health Coalition, an incredible organization we are collaborating with to end stigma surrounding mental health issues.

On the September Letters site, community members share their experiences, often anonymously, by submitting letters about the things that have challenged them, shaped them, made them laugh and cry, and caused them to grow. We are indebted to every individual who has shared their story. We are also proud of every person who has taken the time to visit the site and read a letter. Because telling your story, and reading another's, can change lives.

Writing a letter might feel like an ancient exercise. In truth, it's alive and well. Whether by tapping on our phones or jotting down thoughts with pen and paper, magic happens when we take the time to document our experiences in words. We gain perspective and self-knowledge. We recognize how far we have come. We grow stronger. We gain the fortitude to step in a new direction.

We all want to feel seen. We all want acceptance. We all want love. And we all want to claim our place in this wild world.

Whatever letter-writing may mean to you, we hope in picking up this book you find solace, comfort, and connection. You'll find wisdom and insight here from leading mental health experts, as well as from dear friends and September Letters community members. We have learned so much from everyone who has been generous enough to share—and we want to pass it on. Perhaps in reading this you will find the inspiration to write your own story.

Thank you for reading ours.

We can't wait to read yours.

Love,

Bill + Jaspre

How This Book Works

We organized this book around emotions. This isn't to put any pressure on what you might feel when writing or reading a letter. That's up to you. Rather, we wanted to provide you a compass—one to help you navigate whatever you might be experiencing on any given day. If you are feeling anxious, perhaps flipping to that chapter will offer you solace. Joyful and happy? That chapter offers a place to revel in those feelings.

These pages brim with actual letters and the potential that letter-writing holds. You'll find written letters, scribbled letters, typed letters. You'll see notes and ideas. Stories that we have collected from community members, friends, and public figures whose words have inspired us, and even sparked viral movements.

This book also contains wisdom from minds and hearts we admire. We consulted with experts from a variety of fields, including mental health, the arts, and the sciences, for their thoughts on the power and importance of letter-writing as an act of healing, connection, and self-expression.

Our hope is that this book is like a friend to you, one that you can read, dog-ear, mark up, and look to for insight. It is meant to support and inspire. It is also meant to encourage you to write your own letter—whether that's in the form of a note to someone that you may or may not intend to send, a quick affirmation on a Post-it Note that you keep on your desk for daily inspiration, or a journal entry where you record your deepest thoughts and feelings.

And keep flipping . . . you'll find a little secret pocket in the back. Inspired by Britt's full-circle moment with the girl in the coffee shop, this little nook is meant to keep your letters and Post-it Notes safe.

....

REMEMBER: *Your letter may just be the hope you or someone else needs to make it through to the next challenge, next discovery, next lesson—and the next September.*

....

Dear September	*Letters From Friends*	Q+A EXPERT INTERVIEW	In Their Words...
From our SL Community	*From People We Love*	*Expert Advice*	*Wise Insights*

Hey! :)

This is youR guide of symbols

Be on the lookout

—B & J

" Joy is your
birthright. "

—GRACE HARRY

CHAPTER ONE

Joy + Happiness

Dear Friend Corona . . .

AT THE HEIGHT OF THE COVID-19 PANDEMIC, *an eight-year-old boy named Corona de Vries was being bullied because of his name. When Corona learned that Tom Hanks had tested positive for the virus, he wrote a letter to the famed actor. Tom wrote back to Corona, and with his correspondence he included a photo of the typewriter he'd used to write his response. Reading this note offers a moment of pure joy. It was, and continues to be, a beacon of light and hope during dark times. This is a good old fashioned pen pal correspondence, and we just love it.* **x Jaspre**

10 April 2020

Dear Friend Corona,

    Your letter made my wife and I feel
so wonderful! Thank you for being such a
good friend - friends make their friends
feel good when they are down.

    I saw you on TV, even though I was
back in the USA already - and all healthy.
Even though I was no longer sick, getting
your letter made me feel even better. You
know, you are the only person I've ever
known to have the name Corona - like the
ring around the sun, a crown.

    I thought this typewriter would suit
you. I had taken it to the Gold Coast, and
now, it is back - with you. Ask a grown up
how it works. And use it to write me back.

PS.
You got A friend
in ME!
    T

Thanks again
    T

Dear September

FOR ME, HAPPINESS IS JUST LIKE THE STARS. HOW?
OKAY, PICTURE THIS.

WHAT IF EVERY STAR RESEMBLES A FUNNY, CUTE,
POSITIVE, HAPPY, JOYFUL, CONTENT, OR SATISFYING
MOMENT OF THE DAY. CAUSING THE NIGHT SKY TO SHOW
HOW MUCH HAPPINESS THERE HAS BEEN DURING THE DAY.
I KNOW THAT THERE ARE NIGHTS WHEN THE SKY IS FULL
OF STARS AND ALSO NIGHTS WHEN THERE ARE ONLY A FEW
OR THE CLOUDS CAN EVEN MAKE THEM UNNOTICEABLE. I
DON'T FEEL LIKE THAT'S A BAD OR SAD THING. EVEN WHEN
THERE'S ONLY ONE SHINING STAR... I STILL CHERISH AND
EMBRACE THAT MOMENT OF HAPPINESS I HAD DURING THE
DAY. TOO VALUABLE TO NOT BE ACKNOWLEDGED. AND EVEN
IF THERE ARE NO STARS VISIBLE... THERE'S ALWAYS THE
NEXT DAY. MAYBE IN THE UPCOMING NIGHT THERE WILL
BE (MORE) STARS. THEREFORE (MORE) HAPPINESS!

ENJOY THE STARGAZING!

HAPPY FRIENDLY GREETINGS,
KIM

I used to be so scared of not being liked, I used to be so scared of not being good enough. But I have since learned that only love exists. Anything outside of love is just fear.

In the Universe, the bigger picture, even that fear is just an illusion. Only the love is real, only the love was ever real—in any situation.

It is easier to forgive someone their unkindness when we recognize that it comes from their fear. It is easy to forgive your own behavior, the stuff you're not proud of, when you see it as a product of your fear.

Love is all there is. When I'm feeling out of sync and forgetful of this I write a note to myself: "I am willing to see this differently." And every time I wind up looking again, seeing something new. Ask to see the light in any situation, some situations may take longer than others, but eventually you will.

It costs nothing to share love. Be that person who makes someone else feel confident in your presence. When they feel confident, you feel confident. We are all connected.

And when I am struggling with self-love, when I am down on my body and in a space of self-loathing, when I am intimidated by all the ways society and social media teaches us to be insecure in our own skin, I remind myself of this beautiful quote from one of my favorite books, Women Who Run with the Wolves by Clarissa Pinkola Estés, from the chapter called Joyous Body: The Wild Flesh:

"If she is taught to hate her own body, how can she love her mother's body that has the same configuration as hers? Her grandmother's body, the bodies of her daughters as well? How can she love the bodies of other women (and men) close to her who have inherited the body shapes and configurations of their ancestors?

To attack a woman thusly destroys her rightful pride of affiliation with her own people and robs her of the natural lilt she feels in her body no matter what height, size, shape she is. In essence, the attack on women's bodies is a far-reaching attack on the ones who have gone before her as well as the ones who will come after her."

I would never bash my mother's body, my grandmother's body, or my future daughter's body; so why would I bash my own?

—Torrey DeVitto

Torrey is one of the strongest & most inspiring people I know. This was also our VERY first September Letter! ♥ -B

Torrey DeVitto, actor, producer, and activist

When I hear the word JOY I think of simple things such as a child's life, coffee, a sunny day, petting a dog, etc.

The good thing about joy is it can come in many different shapes and sizes throughout the day. A simple name appearing on your phone can cause you joy or someone giving you the last cookie.

I believe every day (even the really crappy ones) at least one thing will bring you joy and you may not even realize it. Too often we look at all the negative going on around us and forget to appreciate the little things that tend to cause us joy.

Personally, I enjoy looking into what causes people joy. I love seeing the look overtake someone's face when they are having a peaceful, joyful, content moment. I can admit I am a kid at heart. I still get joy just sitting on a swing outside taking in the world. On the other hand, I may feel joy from reading a certain line in a book. I reckon what I am trying to say is ... don't be afraid to take a step back and breathe. Figure out these joyful moments you get to have each and every day and just let time slow down. We are always in such a rush.

Linda

Am I happy? I mean, I'm not unhappy, but that's not exactly the same thing, is it?

I often think that I will never be happy, that I don't have it in me to be happy. Bear with me, it's not as depressing as it sounds, I promise.

I've done some research on happiness—because that's what you do when you have a hard time understanding everyday concepts that seem to come easier for others—and in most definitions I found, it boils down to something like,

"Happiness is an emotional state characterized by feelings of joy, satisfaction, contentment, and fulfillment."

I can feel joy, and to some degree satisfaction, but I have a hard time with the last two.

There's this conventional idea of happiness as a perfect picture, as a synonym of having it all, as an end goal.

But what if we don't have an end goal? What if we won't ever be content? What if we don't fit in the conventional picture of happiness? What if we simply don't all experience happiness in the same way?

I figured I don't have to fit the mold, which I clearly don't. I don't care that people find it odd how much I enjoy my solitude, I don't care if I fit this preconceived idea of what's normal for a certain age or gender or whatever, and I certainly don't feel this urge to pursue happiness. Happiness feels like such a large, abstract, definitive concept to me...So, I choose not to look at it that way.

I try to focus on doing things that bring me pleasure and joy, things that warm my heart, even if momentarily, even if they don't make me feel contentment or satisfaction, even if they don't last long, even if they're not perfect.

I don't know much about happiness, but the way I try to contribute to other people's happiness is by not making things harder for them. People say I have a good temper—I don't, I just think we're all dealing with so much crap that the last thing I want is to negatively add to it. So, I try to be kind and compassionate and patient and supportive.

And what I realized is that maybe the way for happiness is by showing the same kindness, compassion, patience, and support for myself. Maybe for me, happiness is no more than not being at war with myself.

Filipa

DREW,

It's a foggy Monday morning, and the cool fall air—your favorite!—is drifting through the window. The garbage truck is making its morning rounds, clattering down the street. It's distracting but the break in stillness is comforting.

At this moment, I'm in my midtown Manhattan apartment that I share with my loving boyfriend. Three years into our relationship, I have never felt so safe, secure, and happy. This is the first romantic relationship I've had, but I'm now experiencing the joy I never knew possible when I was your age. If only you could see years ahead and save yourself so much pain.

Yes, I did say boyfriend. And yes, this is on the Internet for all the world to see.
I know your heart is racing and you're frantically trying to figure out how to delete this. You're terrified of being found out. But let me tell you something—you are gay. Andrew Gelwicks is gay, gay, gay. And you know what? What you will come to see is that your queerness is the very best thing that will ever happen to you.

You can turn down the temperature dial on your constantly boiling resentment. The things you are currently hating most about yourself will turn out to be the mighty foundation for your wonderful life. In the secrecy of your bedroom, you now spend hours fashioning Mom's tablecloths into dresses and adorning yourself with your sister's jewelry. But these unique skills will become your career as a celebrity fashion stylist. You will get to dress the most extraordinary, talented, beautiful people in the finest clothing—for a living!

And do you remember all those short stories and "books" you wrote in school, that you tried to get "published"? Well, you've finally done it.

The painful moments you are experiencing now—questioning your every thought and movement, practicing lowering your voice, hiding in your darkened bedroom for hours at a time, sleeping fitfully at night with questions and fears—your self-loathing is destructive and unnecessary. You are not broken, you are not wrong. Not at all. A vibrantly beautiful future lies before you.

The trials you are now enduring are building you. You are becoming stronger, more passionate, more fearless, more empathetic, more driven. The fragile, thin roots that now barely connect you to this world are growing stronger and deeper, anchoring you in ways you may not recognize in the whirl of daily life.

Don't stop believing in what is possible. I am living a life you cannot now envision could ever be. What you are going through is not easy. But know this: your current struggles are developing into tremendous strengths.

I can't wait until you get here.

—Andrew

Andrew Gelwicks, stylist and writer

Joy Conditioning and Saying "I Love You"

with Dr. Wendy Suzuki

Professor of Neural Science and Psychology and Dean of the College of Arts & Science at New York University

WENDY SUZUKI, PHD, *is a professor of neural science and psychology at New York University, where she specializes in brain plasticity. I've long been fascinated by Dr. Suzuki's research, which focuses on how our brains form and retain new memories. But what really struck me was a story she told about how she and her family members all began to say "I love you" to one another after her father was diagnosed with Alzheimer's disease. "I love you" became the three words that Dr. Suzuki's dad always remembered to say. It was an honor to talk about this and more with Dr. Suzuki.* **x Britt**

BRITT: How has sharing a story helped you in either your personal life or your research?

DR. WENDY SUZUKI: Probably the most personally impactful story that I have shared was at The Moth talk that I did about my family deciding to start saying "I love you." After my father developed dementia, I had this realization that in our family, we loved each other but we never said "I love you" to each other. This story was about the time I decided to start saying "I love you" to my parents. It was weird to suddenly start doing this one day when we'd never done it before.

Since sharing this story, I can't tell you the number of people who have come up to me and said, "I don't say I love you to my parents either! You have inspired me to know that it's possible to start."

BRITT: Did you find that you saying "I love you" to your parents changed your life in any specific way? Did it affect your father's experience with Alzheimer's?

WENDY: It changed my life extraordinarily. To this day, every time I talk to my mom we always say "I love you" at the end of a conversation. I always think back to the time when we didn't say it, or even think about saying it. It changed my dad because saying "I love you" was one of the things that he would always remember, without prompting, at the end of our conversations. I didn't have to remind him. I would be ready to explain it to him, "Okay, remember, Dad, what we decided . . ." But no, he always remembered to say it, even when his memory was bad at the end.

BRITT: Do you think that somehow the emotion of love was able to override what was happening in his brain?

WENDY: This is the way I explain it from the perspective of neuroscience: One of my first areas of study was how human memory works. We've known for a long time that emotional resonance is a big booster to our normal everyday memory. We tend to remember the happiest moments and the saddest moments of our lives more vividly because of emotional resonance.

The way I think of it is that my father had never been asked permission by his daughter to say, "I love you," so when I asked, that was a memorable moment in his life because it was full of emotion for him and for all of us. I say we beat Alzheimer's that day, because he was able to form this memory that lasted until he passed away.

BRITT: How is it beneficial for people to tell their stories and share them with others?

WENDY: By retelling our most important stories, those that we want to remember, we are restrengthening those memories. For me, this process is very helpful, and in my newest book, *Good Anxiety*, I talk about a tool I've invented called "joy conditioning," which is designed specifically to counteract "fear conditioning." Fear conditioning happens to all of us. An example of fear conditioning is the time when I was living in Washington, DC, and my apartment was burgled. I can still remember walking around the corner—my door was the last one on the hallway—and seeing my door crowbarred open. I remember it so vividly because of fear conditioning. Dangerous moments are automatically encoded to protect us in the future, which is great. But then you realize, "I'm walking around with all of this fear."

Similarly, each time you repeat a beautiful story, like my story of saying "I love you" to my parents, that memory becomes stronger, and you relive those emotions. That's joy conditioning—going back and culling your memories for the most joyful, the happiest, the funniest things, and reaffirming them.

Joy conditioning is going back and explicitly reliving those happy memories, to get the good emotions that are already in our memory banks and put them into a more active state.

BY WRITING DOWN YOUR THOUGHTS, YOU GAIN PERSPECTIVE AND START TO UNDERSTAND YOURSELF BETTER.

Exploring an Overlooked Element of Happiness

with Gretchen Rubin
....
Author

WHAT MAKES US TRULY HAPPY? *It's a question that has long intrigued Gretchen Rubin, a former lawyer and best-selling author. Rubin's work, which includes the wildly successful books* The Happiness Project *and* The Happiness Project *journal series (to name a few), has had a huge influence on us at September Letters. There is nothing conventional about her approach. Gretchen's outlook and take on happiness and joy are totally unique. But one aspect that really lands for us is her approach to journaling toward happiness, which mirrors our belief in letter-writing. Gretchen believes that the key is to take control of your narrative and use that authentic story about yourself to reach others. Britt and I loved having the chance to connect with Gretchen.* **x Jaspre**

JASPRE: Gretchen, thanks for speaking with us. Would you start by telling us what happiness means to you? I know it's a big word.

GRETCHEN: It is a big word, and in fact I never define it because I started my career in law, where I spent an entire semester arguing about the definition of "contract." And happiness is even more elusive! There are something like fifteen academic definitions of happiness, and people just really want to say to you, "Well, happiness means this, but joy means this, and bliss means this." I like the fact that happiness is a big enough term that we can all bring to it what we want.

JASPRE: Let's talk a bit about *The Happiness Toolbox* that you created as a companion to your book, *The Happiness Project*, and how writing in a journal is a big part of that toolbox. Why is keeping a journal important to you, and why is it a critical part of your work?

GRETCHEN: Keeping a journal is a tool that can serve many functions. For some people, it's an opportunity for self-reflection. By writing down your thoughts, you gain perspective and start to understand yourself better, and you gain insights that may have eluded you when you were stuck in your own head.

Keeping a journal can also give a feeling of control. There's a lot of research showing that when people write down what's happening to them, especially if they're in a difficult or challenging situation, they gain a sense of control—partly from that sense of perspective, and partly from the tendency to make meaning out of what's happening. For people who worry a lot and ruminate, writing things down is very helpful because your brain thinks, "Okay, cool, that's all taken care of, I can think about other things now." If you haven't written it down, it's like the brain keeps trying to make sure: "Don't forget, don't forget! What about this? What about that?" But by writing in a journal, your thoughts are memorialized in a way that relieves anxiety. That gives us a feeling of control, and feeling control is really one of the most important elements of happiness.

JASPRE: Do you keep a journal?

GRETCHEN: Yes, I like to experiment with different kinds of aspects of keeping a journal. I write memoir, which involves memorializing my thoughts and feelings. I'm constantly using writing to process what I'm doing. I have a blog, and for eight years I wrote on that every single day, which was a form of keeping a journal. I do think there's a distinction between keeping public journal—even if it's online and only two people are reading it—and keeping a private journal where you record your deepest, most private thoughts. I keep some journals that are my deepest, most private thoughts and reflections. But I'm also very drawn to using my own experience as a way to connect with other people, which is a different way to use a journal. I think that's the reason that a lot of people are drawn to writing online.

JASPRE: Would you agree that a big part of happiness comes from owning and rewriting your story?

GRETCHEN: Oh, yes. Reframing your story makes a huge difference. Here's a great example: When my daughters were little, I had to take them to doctors' appointments all the time. I remember one day complaining to my mother about it. I should also mention that my in-laws lived right around the corner from us, and my mother-in-law, Judy, was very involved with the kids. So, as I was complaining, my mother suggested, "Maybe Judy would take the girls to the doctor for you." My immediate response was, "Oh no, I want to do it!" And I realized, "I don't have to do it. I get to do it." I did not for one minute want to give it up. I actually wanted to do it much more than I had realized. My mother's suggestion made me see that. I get to do it.

How to Pursue
the Positive Emotion

with Grace Harry
....

Joy Strategist

"Joy is your birthright."

JOY CAN SOMETIMES FEEL ELUSIVE. *What does it mean to feel joy? Does joy visit you or do you conjure it? In our wild world, feeling joy can seem like a far-off idea, something that's impossible to have or feel on a regular basis. But joy strategist and activist Grace Harry believes the opposite. Grace, who left her high-powered career as a music executive to help people infuse more joy in their lives, believes that this feeling is something we each have in our heart and can find in all our days, no matter how hard life is. If there ever was a tangible rainbow, Grace is it, and I just love her for it.* **x Jaspre**

JASPRE: What is joy to you?

GRACE: Joy is a feeling. It's an emotion from your heart. It's our birthright. It's our home—depending on what your spiritual faith is.

Right now, people are so overwhelmed with life. But the more you can do things to fan the flame of your heart and keep that joy alive will not only keep your mental health in a beautiful space, it will also really change your entire physicality.

JASPRE: That's amazing. Is there a difference between happiness and joy?

GRACE: Oh, yes.

JASPRE: When editors reach out to you, they say, "let's talk about happiness." And you say, "let's talk about joy."

GRACE: I want people to see that happiness is a concept developed from our understanding of how we're supposed to behave. That behavior is based on the state of mind that works for our system—in our case, a productivity-obsessed culture. Whereas with joy, you see a one-day-old human and they're smiling because they are joyful. We all have joy. It's in our heart. It's who we are.

JASPRE: The world is a tough place. People are going through radical change. For someone who wants to feel joy but is having a hard time getting there, what's your advice?

GRACE: What's complicated about joy and happiness and pleasure is that the heart steps up as the first boss in the body. People think it's the brain, but the heart jumps online first.

There are things that happen to us preverbally that our heart feels, and these things can feel uncomfortable. If I told you, "You're going to get a tattoo," we would have had a verbal description and conversation to help us understand what it's going to look like, what it's going to feel like, and what we're signing up for. But when we do things intimately, our heart is taking the lead, and sometimes we feel pain that we don't understand. But we have the choice at that moment to change the way we feel by accessing joy.

We can access joy in many ways. If I'm really feeling mean, sometimes I just say "bad thoughts be gone" like I'm sweeping them out like garbage. When a negative state really gets a hold of me, I have a whole bunch of practices. It can be thinking of something that makes me feel invincible or listening to a song that has a message in it. Or even listening to a silly song—and I know I've tortured you with my SpongeBob song over and over and over! Sometimes you can look at an *SNL* clip or a comedy moment or read a joke. You can jump up and down or dance.

JASPRE: You refer to things called "joy snacks." What are those?

GRACE: Let's say we're going on a long journey where there's not going to be any food or water. We know it's essential that we pack sustenance so that we can ration it for the whole journey. But we don't live our everyday lives that way. No matter what your morning routine might be, you're going to go outside and be entangled with other

---

HERE ARE TWO JOY SNACK PRACTICES YOU CAN DO:

1. **TAKE A TALISMAN WITH YOU DURING THE DAY.** If you have emotions, thoughts, or feelings that are toiling in your brain, or if you have a hard time processing energy around you, have a talisman that reminds you to ground. The practice of rosaries and mala beads are tools to keep you on track as you touch each bead with prayer, meditation, or chant. Yet we don't need something that someone else has created. A talisman can be anything that reminds you to get quiet and go in when you hold it. This could be a drawing you love. It could be a picture, even one of yourself where you can see the moment you were in a beautiful space. You can look into your eyes and realign with that feeling.

2. **MOVE YOUR BODY.** You can put on one song—a song that makes you feel expansive and fantastic. Then go wild. Jump around. Move. If you're in an office space, go into a bathroom stall. Or sit at your desk and move your shoulders around. You don't need a lot of time for this. Just take a moment to breathe.

energies—other human energies, animal energies, things that could really put a damper on your mood or change your state of mind. So you have to start being prepared to support your energy by making sure you have joy snacks, which are things or practices that nourish us and bring us joy and happiness.

The importance of joy snacks is to not hold things in your body. They're about making sure that you plan how to sustain, support, curate, cultivate, and be juicy with your joy all day. How can you fan the flame of your heart so that when you come home at the end of the day you feel great and haven't let the world deplete you? My answer: joy snacks.

JASPRE: One of my favorite joy snacks of yours is the "ME" book.

GRACE: I have so much to say about the "ME" book.

JASPRE: Talk to us about the "ME" book. It's relevant to September Letters because we want to honor all different types of writing. It may not always be an ink-to-paper letter. It could be a text. It could be a drawing . . .

GRACE: I used to think how weird it was when I would go into a meeting with a fresh notebook, because that was "business Grace." Whereas when I'm at home, I write my dreams in my dream journal. I thought: That's why I feel so divided in my own reality of life. I approach my professional life in one way and my personal life in another. At the time, I had things going on in my life that made me feel far from my badass Grace, that eleven-year-old child inside of me with vivid dreams. So I started adding stickers and drawing art in my notebooks. Then I had my eureka moment: This was my "ME" book. This came from inside of me. My beating heart, my vision board. A place for dreams and ideas. So I started writing my "ME" book. And anytime anyone said something to me that I felt really changed me, I wrote it down and I would draw around it for days.

Every time I open a page, I see that I've channeled and infused so much joy and true Grace in there. So much juiciness and excitement. When I'm having a meeting, I take the "ME" book now—it's already infused with that much magic. That's why the "ME" book is so important. It doesn't matter the size. It doesn't matter how many pages. It is the energy of it.

It's been so helpful for me, professionally and personally, to stay on course with my big dreams, because they're all in this little book of ME.

AN EASY PRACTICE FOR WHEN YOU'RE IN A JOYLESS HOLE

While you're walking around your world, perhaps getting ready to go out or just brushing your teeth, put a new spin on the gratitude list: Start saying things you're grateful for to yourself—even the silliest, most banal things. "List hundreds of gratitudes weven," says Grace. The key behind this? It will spark humor and joy. "It's going to start to make you laugh at yourself when you get to your gratitude for your own cells and atoms." But keep cycling through them, says Grace.

Okay, here it goes.

I was about sixteen when I figured out I was gay and I was struggling a bit to accept it, still coming to terms with it, when the kids at my school spread the rumor. A few months later, my mother found out and she didn't really take it the way I wished her to.

I was sixteen and people just sort of took the chance to talk about who I was away from me, so I stopped talking. Not completely, but over the years I settled for small talks until I stopped discussing my feelings even with my friends.

I became this shell of a person at one point, and I felt alone and worthless for so long. I kept thinking, "If not even my mother can accept who I am, then what's the point?" and I got in a spiral of suicidal thoughts I couldn't get out of.

I don't know when it happened exactly, but something clicked in me. I knew I couldn't keep it up and I knew I needed some support; it didn't matter how afraid I was of talking about myself. I opened up with an online friend, because I found writing so much easier than speaking, but it helped me a lot. Even writing to no one in particular helped, actually—it was a start. Then one night I got the courage to confront my mom about it. We talked and talked and talked, and I found out she felt guilty for what she said to me years ago, and she said something I wanna say to whoever is reading this: you have to do what is right for you, what makes YOU happy. Even if you feel your happiness might hurt someone else, you cannot keep trying to meet everyone's expectations. I know it's not easy, but it is possible to put yourself first.

I promise you, the place you're at, all the loneliness you feel, the will to disappear: that's not the finish line. You will be brave. You will open up. You will feel better, one day at a time, and you will feel like yourself. I'm twenty-four now and I'm coming out of that shell just now. It's not too late, it's never too late.

I believe you can do it, too.

Love,
Mau

Find your joy
Let it infuse your purpose.
Expect mistakes
Let them teach you wisdom.
Embrace honesty
It will gift you intimacy

Lean into grief
It will deepen your love
Slow down
Find solace in solitude.
Listen
Your gut is your guide.
Connect
We are meant to lean on each other

Kelley Jakle, singer-songwriter and actor

"At a time when so many of us are isolated, a letter is a whisper in the heart that we are never truly alone."

—DIANA CHAO

CHAPTER TWO

Resilience + Healing

___

My name is Britt Snow. For as long as I can remember, I've been a sensitive person. As a kid, my quirks included not being able to walk if there was a wrinkle in my socks. I would cry every day at not only the thought of a car crash, but the sight of a butterfly. I felt... everything. I struggled with depression, anxiety, and an eating disorder for most of my early life. I started dieting at thirteen years old and became anorexic by age fifteen, the same age I started obsessive and self-harmful behaviors.

These destructive behaviors lasted throughout my teen years. In my early twenties, I suffered from an anxiety disorder that made it hard for me to speak in public. Because of my panic attacks I had to quit acting from ages twenty-three to twenty-five. I thought I would never work again. I would shake uncontrollably and my throat would suddenly close if I tried to speak with anyone other than my close friends or family. I didn't understand what was happening to me or why my body was shutting down. I believed in myself, I knew I was good at my job, yet I couldn't do the very thing that I felt defined me. It took me two years without the tether and validation of my career to finally start to heal. I thought I would never be able to be a "normal" person, someone without some sort of disease or crutch.

I now have fourteen years of recovery from all harmful behaviors. It took many meetings, therapists, countless books, breakdowns, mess-ups, sponsors, healers, and beautiful friends to get me through. I couldn't be more grateful for my story because it prepared me for the life I have now. There were moments I wasn't sure if I would be here and somehow here I am. This was due to a tiny voice inside my head that told me, "Don't give up—one day this will help someone."

I still struggle with depression and anxiety today, but I've learned to value it. I accept how sensitive I am. I appreciate how colorful and vibrant the world feels to me. The pain and anxiety I feel, while sometimes overwhelming, always teach me something. I have the tools now to work through those feelings. Though it may be harder, longer, and more uncomfortable, it is always more worthwhile.

I know I'm not alone, I know I'm one of many, and I know my struggles are not better or worse than anyone else's—they are our own and they all matter collectively.

My letter to September is addressed to the person who is still struggling. I never, ever thought I would get through. I hope you know you are not alone. Keep going.

More importantly, I hope you trust and listen to the voice that tells you: There is so much more to discover and so much more to your story. Telling it matters.

Writing Letters to Heal Ourselves

with Ana Tucker

Board Certified Hypnotherapist, Master Neurolinguistic Programming (NLP) Practitioner, and a Licensed Clinical Social Worker

ANA TUCKER *deeply transformed my life and has given me a tool in my toolbox that I consistently turn to. A revered hypnotherapist and neuro-linguistic practitioner, Ana is deeply intuitive in her work helping people to move past trauma toward a state of balance and healing. Britt and I share a passion for hypnotherapy, so it felt like a homecoming to talk with Ana about how she incorporates letter-writing, a practice she finds to be deeply transformative for her clients and herself. Ana told us that writing, particularly letter-writing, is so powerful because it "puts us in a state of trance," not unlike the state of hypnotherapy itself.* **x Jaspre**

JASPRE: You use letter-writing as a tool in your work with your clients. But first, how has this practice been impactful for you, personally?

ANA: I have to say, I've used letter-writing even more since submitting my own September Letter. Following the format of "Dear September" was profound for me. It showed me how often healers also need healing. Often we're too busy healing those around us to notice when we need to look inward ourselves. Letter-writing has allowed me to bring together these discordant parts of my life. It was in the middle of COVID when I started to write letters to myself, and it helped me make sense of some experiences that I've had both recently and in the past. It also connected me with an early memory that I realized set me on my path to healing. It blew me away.

JASPRE: How do you find letter-writing to be powerful for your clients?

ANA: When we're writing there's an intention behind what we're doing. When we're writing a letter to ourselves or to the world about a life experience, there's something that's being expressed. This brings about a state of trance, which is a focused relaxation. Writing is the tool and behind it is an intent to express something. That combination allows letter-writing to become therapeutic and to become a way of directly communicating with the subconscious mind, the powerful mind, the emotional self. By doing that we can do amazing, miraculous things. We can heal wounds. We can bring our shame or rage out into the light. All of this allows us to clear out our psyche and make room to bring in what we want to bring in.

JASPRE: In my experience with hypnotherapy, it's been about my subconscious mind but also a story that's attached to it. How does hypnotherapy help us realize and understand the stories in our minds?

Our stories come from our beliefs about ourselves and the world around us.

ANA: We don't live our desires, we live our stories. That is because our stories are held within the subconscious emotional part of our minds. We have around six thousand thoughts during the day. On average, 95 percent of those originate within the subconscious mind. We know how powerful the subconscious mind is, but once we start looking at the magic of the subconscious mind, it gets interesting. We're all telling ourselves a story of some sort. Now this story may work for you. It could be a "you go girl" story in your mind. But often I see that there's a part of the story that's not working. To change that, we need to work with the subconscious mind, which is where every memory is kept, every emotion is held, and our beliefs about ourselves and about the world are locked down.

Our stories come from our beliefs about ourselves and the world around us. So being able to identify and access those stories allows us to change them. In doing that, we change our relationship between our conscious and subconscious. We change ourselves and we change the world around us. The power of letter-writing to change your story is so incredible.

Writing creates a direct path into the subconscious mind to say, "This may be the old story, but I am choosing a new story right here."

JASPRE: What is a writing tool or exercise for supporting our mental health that you recommend?

ANA: I'm a big believer in manifesting. One of the tools that I find most powerful is to be clear about what one wants: knowing what we want and focusing on that as if we already have it. So if there's an aspect of your life, say you'd like more calm in your life or more action in your life, think about that and then write about it in detail. This allows you to focus on it and—most importantly—to bring in the feelings that come with having it. That is powerful because the emotional connection with our goals—when they are aligned with our subconscious beliefs—is where the magic happens.

You can write to your future self, to a person you never finished communicating with, or to someone who's passed away. Whatever needs to be expressed. Own shame. Own guilt. Own something that you feel bad about. In that trance state, we are working directly with the emotional part of the subconscious mind, and that's where the communication happens.

And again, the magic magic magic. 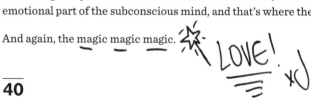 LOVE! xo

It gets better.

That's something you hear a lot. At this point, you probably think it's stupid. Just another expression everybody's heard that's never gonna come true. That's how I felt. If anything, it made me feel worse, more hopeless, as I knew that it was never going to happen.

But now, as I look back on my healing journey, I realized why I perceived it this way. Healing is not linear. You don't wake up one morning and suddenly all your problems are gone. It's in the little things. Maybe you made it a few more minutes. Maybe you got out of bed.

We don't realize how important these things are. Every minute you make it is another minute of progress. Every day you get up is another effort to get better. And then, ever so slowly, it gets easier. Maybe you manage two minutes, even three. Maybe you got out of your bed three days this week. And then without even realizing it, those little things build up. Before you know it, those little things make your life completely different.

The problem is the stigma. Society teaches us that healing happens overnight. It seems as though the second you get help, it all gets better. But that's not the truth. It takes a long time. It's hard, and people don't realize how much effort it takes.

But you know. You've been there.

It's not until you look at how far you've come that you can truly appreciate your progress. It's the little things that are important, that can make a huge difference. So look back, even on the smallest things. Even if they don't seem like much, learn to appreciate them.

I know this won't work for all, but this helped me to have such hope in my healing journey. I guess the goal of this is to help somebody else. Even if it's just one person.

More importantly, I hope you trust and listen to the voice that tells you: There is so much more to discover and so much more to your story. Telling it matters.

—Anonymous

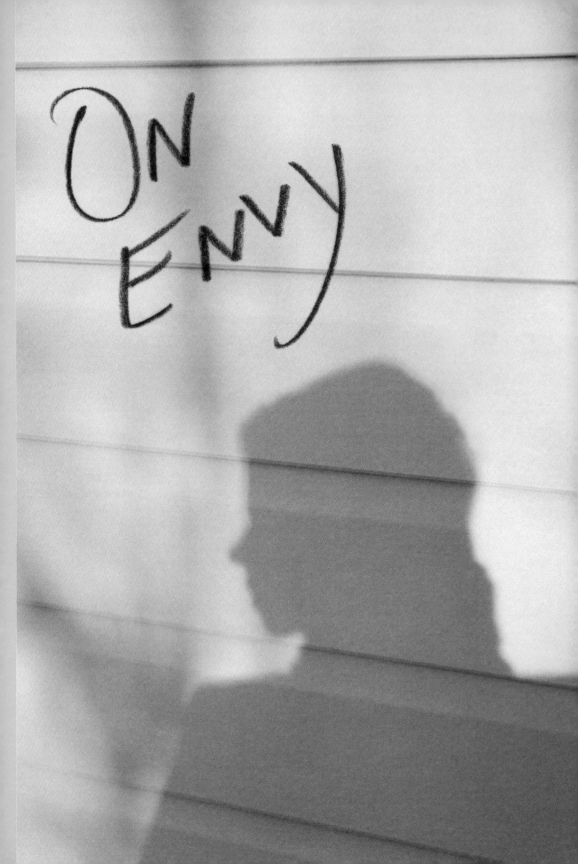

I hold precious space for emotions that are talked about less than others. Those feelings are my favorite to explore as an actor because I have a safe place to work through my own baggage.

To start: We don't talk about envy enough.

In my daily exchanges if someone says, "I'm so jealous of you," I follow it up with some self-deprecating joke about how fill-in-the-blank is not actually that great. Which is often bull****. I'm super happy and proud of my life, and minimizing the discomfort or envy of other people does my happiness and their growth a disservice. Social niceties are weird.

And what about the people I feel jealous of? I've really begun to examine my own feelings of envy. I know it's one thing to know something logically and still have a difficult time processing it emotionally. Trust me...my body loves a mental and emotional deep dive. Still, these questions move me through both a lot faster.

1. WHAT IS IT, SPECIFICALLY, THAT SPARKED THIS FEELING?
   What is the thing, emotion, or quality this person appears to have that you want for yourself?
2. IS THIS ACTUALLY A DREAM OR GOAL OF YOURS? Or has societal messaging or the status quo temporarily abducted your beautiful brain?
3. IF THE ENVY IS VISCERAL, what action steps can you take toward making your dream a reality?
4. IF YOU THINK YOUR DREAM IS IMPOSSIBLE, WHY? How can you work toward both believing in yourself AND learning to ask for help?
5. IF IT'S SOCIETAL MESSAGING, how can you shield or protect yourself while you're temporarily feeling more vulnerable to the messaging?

Listen...I know #4 is another exploration all to itself. Building true confidence and being incredibly resourceful in an increasingly scarce society should be taught in schools IMO.

On jealousy itself, I find that once I can pinpoint the exact trigger, I'm able to push past those feelings a little more efficiently. Like most emotions, it's usually also a cover for something else that needs to be addressed. *Coughs in procrastination.*

Besides, it's beyond perfectly normal and understandable. We're in a moment where it's becoming more and more impossible to decipher what's real and what's not in the lives of other people. It's also become harder to hear our own inner voice and instincts. Time after time, when I give myself the gift of silence, the voice inside me says:

That's not your dream, De. There are only green lights ahead if you stay true to your path.

Listen to yourself.

— DeWanda Wise

Our Relationship to Our Bodies, Food, and the Stories We Tell Ourselves

with Geneen Roth

Author and Teacher

"It's about showing yourself tenderness and kindness."

FOR DECADES, GENEEN ROTH *has explored our messy, complicated, and often fascinating relationships with our bodies, our minds, and food. One of her most famous books,* Women Food and God, *is considered a ray of light in helping so many people—myself included—shift their perspective, release binary labels, and find a sense of inner freedom. Geneen, who is a recovered compulsive eater, writes with a rawness and clarity that hits the reader's soul. In 2019, she started* The Cancer Chronicles, *a platform where she openly shares about her journey with cancer. I was honored to talk to Geneen about how writing and storytelling opens possibilities for dealing with fear and our darkest emotions.* **x Britt**

BRITT: In your books, you write about the stories we tell ourselves and the stories that we repeat. Do you feel it's important that we rewire our stories and view them in a different way, or is it important to write these stories down to connect with others?

GENEEN: The stories we tend to tell other people is often a partial digestion of a story that we tell ourselves. I usually don't write down stories in books or on a social media platform that I haven't sat with first unquestioned. I don't put a raw, unquestioned, emotionally charged thing out there for people because I feel like they will then get the charge of it but not what's fully possible from working with it. I'm interested in the possibilities—and the stories are a way there. The stories we tell ourselves are sometimes based on associations and memories that are from a long time ago, sometimes so long ago they are no longer true.

BRITT: We often wonder at September Letters if it is therapeutic for someone to share a letter about something they haven't fully processed because there may be so much more to their stories that they haven't yet realized.

GENEEN: That's a good point. It is possible to just dig yourself deeper into what's wrong. On the other hand, sometimes I will write for the sake of writing. I will just download what's going on to get it all out. It's like spreading out a quilt that's been all crumpled up. So sometimes I don't know what I really know, or what I really even believe, until I start writing. But that writing is usually for me, and I don't tend to share it.

I have been writing The Cancer Chronicles because I had breast cancer. I wrote about how my mother told me I was fat when I sent her a picture. There was a very big response to that. I had sat with that whole thing of her telling me I was fat and of what that meant to me. I digested it so that what I put out in that post wasn't, "Can you believe my mother told me I was fat?" I don't think it's healing to blame anyone. The real question was: What did I do with my mother telling me I was fat?

So it's important to me when I put something out for other people to see that I've gone as far as I can go in that moment and that I'm not putting more blame and victimhood and charge and rage and fear out there.

BRITT: You talk about the awareness that it takes to just be with your body and in the moment. That can be helpful for someone who compulsively eats, to take the moment to just be with the feelings. Are there tools to be less reactive when we hear old stories or hurtful things?

GENEEN: It's a practice. It's a process of forgetting and remembering, forgetting and remembering. It's about understanding that any story you're telling yourself, or that you're hearing, that brings you suffering, needs to be questioned. How do you know you are suffering? Your chest contracts. Your stomach drops. You feel like you may collapse. You feel two-inches tall. Or you get furious. So that first step is to realize something's going on and it's never about out there. It's never about what your mother said. It's about how what your mother said connects with what you believe.

The thing that I teach is how to turn toward, not away, from yourself. If you feel you need comfort right away and so you look to food, that's turning away from yourself. That is not being with yourself; that's leaving yourself. You're basically abandoning yourself. It must be about scooping yourself up. It's about showing yourself tenderness and kindness.

BRITT: One of my favorite quotes of yours is, "Our relationship to food is the exact microcosm of our relationship to life itself." What have you learned about the soul and giving back and how has that changed your journey to eating recovery?

GENEEN: What I often say about my relationship with food is what Laura Davis, who cowrote The Courage to Heal, said about surviving sexual abuse: Once you have been a compulsive eater, you don't go back to not being a compulsive eater until and unless your identity shifts into vastness and spaciousness and spirit so that you don't identify with being a compulsive eater anymore. You don't take yourself to be that. You know that's part of you, but it is not all of you. It is certainly not the truest part of you. Food is still a raw nerve for me. It's not about losing weight and gaining weight. But still, if I find myself wanting to eat when I'm not hungry I think: What's really going on?

Can I accept myself?

The strongest thing I've ever done for myself is to acknowledge and accept my weaknesses. That they are part of me. That it's okay to be vulnerable, to need help. That you'll be fine to walk around without a shield or an armor. That you can show your true self. It makes absolutely no difference what people think of you. It's a strength I'm called to bring out every day.

To accept ourselves for who we are, not for who we think the world wants us to be.

There is a line in a poem by Rumi that resonates with me. "His infirmity is of the body, not of the Spirit: the weakness lies in the ark, not in Noah."

There are many cracks in our bodies, in our beings, whether physical, mental, emotional. Flaws that come with the package. We can aim to heal through work, therapy, knowledge, experience, help from others, etc. . . . But ultimately, it is our essence that remains and has always been who we truly are. It's scary to acknowledge that and bring out the pure unprotected part of ourselves. Are we strong enough to show it to the world? Are we okay if everyone sees us for who we truly are? Can I accept myself?

The strongest thing I do every day is to find those moments where I am brave enough to drop the protective layer that helps me "function" in the world.

Santiago

Santiago Cabrera, actor

THE STRONGEST THING
I'VE EVER DONE FOR
MYSELF WAS TO PUSH
THROUGH MY EXCUSES AND
WHAT-IFS ABOUT THERAPY
AND ACTUALLY BOOK MY
FIRST APPOINTMENT.

Sam Richardson,
actor and producer

Finding Catharsis in Writing to People She Doesn't Know

with Diana Chao

Founder and Executive Director at Letters to Strangers

DIANA CHAO *was a high school sophomore living below the poverty line when she started writing letters to people she didn't know. Chao, a first-generation Buyi Chinese American, had been diagnosed with bipolar disorder and a blinding eye disease only years prior. She wanted a way to connect. To feel seen. To love. So she picked up her pen—and her nonprofit, Letters to Strangers, was born. Here she walks us through the origin story of Letters to Strangers, now the largest global youth-for-youth mental health nonprofit. "The most rewarding aspect of creating this community has been the stories," Chao tells us. "Not just stories of people coming back from the brink after they read a letter, though of course those are meaningful and humbling beyond words. But also, the stories of everyday people, of all backgrounds, sharing their vulnerabilities with a stranger—putting that trust in humanity to listen, to care, and to feel those emotions, too."* **xx Britt and Jaspre**

BRITT AND JASPRE: What have you learned about yourself from creating the Letters to Strangers community?

DIANA: When my little brother found me after my final suicide attempt, I made a vow: I was going to do everything I could to start to heal, if not for my sake, then for his. So I started exploring protective techniques that anyone can do anywhere—journaling, making art, etc. It was around this time that I started writing letters. I was too ashamed and terrified of my illness to tell others about it, so I wrote to strangers. As I wrote to these people I'd never met, I thought: How is it that I can be so empathetic to these people I'll never see, but I can't give the same love to myself? Did I not deserve the same? The more I wrote the letters, the more I started to recognize my own voice and worth. I started to believe that writing is humanity distilled into ink.

So powerful ♡ -B
:)

BRITT AND JASPRE: How has writing served as a tool for healing throughout your mental health journey?

DIANA: Writing has been a grounding tool, particularly when I'm holding a pen and paper in my hands. It's a conduit for my mind when I start to think astray, and I can ink my thoughts down before they run too far away. Writing letters, in particular, has been helpful because sometimes journaling itself can trigger a negative inward spiral when it's just me and my thoughts. When I'm writing to someone, I have to remain conscious of where my words are headed. That awareness allows me insight and empathy toward myself in a way that I haven't been able to find elsewhere.

BRITT AND JASPRE: You've openly written about your bipolar diagnosis. How have you seen this admission impact those in your community?

DIANA: When I first started sharing my diagnosis, it was within the Letters to Strangers community of youths for youths. Not only has it felt empowering for me and—to my humbling knowledge—others as well, it has meant a lot to girls and nonbinary people of color. I remember so many fellow Asian Americans thanking me for showing them that it's okay to have a mental illness, and that it doesn't mean there is something wrong with us or that we are being ungrateful or that we just need to drink some herbal tea. We are all human beings, and that means we all go through ups and downs. Normalizing talking about emotions, seeking preventive care and strategies, practicing healthy communication with others and ourselves—these are all things I am so grateful to be able to teach others and continuously learn and develop in my own life.

BRITT AND JASPRE: How does writing a letter to a stranger differ from writing a letter to a close friend?

DIANA: Sometimes the hardest conversations to have are with our friends. We worry about their reactions, that we're being "Debbie Downers," that this might come back to bite us in the future. The truth is that the people we know well also already know us well, and that can be scary. Besides, people near us tend to want to give us advice—out of kindness, sure, but most people are not very good at saying things in gentle ways, and sometimes the last thing we want is to be told that we need to be fixed. Sometimes we just want to be listened to and trusted with autonomy like a fellow human being.

Writing to a stranger is a sort of freedom. You can think of the stranger as the ideal person to talk to: a grandmotherly figure, a child, or a businessperson—it doesn't matter. What matters is that they don't know you, so they will read your story as you feel you must tell it. It doesn't matter if they judge you—you'll never know if they do, anyway.

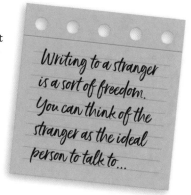

Writing to a stranger is a sort of freedom. You can think of the stranger as the ideal person to talk to...

I take my time to read some of the other wonderful letters that people write and there was one in particular that struck me. I won't name any names, but it inspired me to write this and share it with others.

I may have written a couple other letters before this, but this also concerns an aspect of my life I am fighting vigorously against...all the time.

I'm someone who belittles my body. Who has belittled my own body for most of my life, and admittedly, I still do. To the extent that I've altered my entire intake of food just so I can change it.

Something that many don't know about me is that I have hypothyroidism. My metabolism doesn't work the way it's supposed to, and my thyroid doesn't produce enough hormones. Therefore, I have spent my entire life being "overweight," "bigger than all the other girls around me," and "needing to lose weight"...according to my father and late grandma. I used to believe there was something wrong with me. Why did I need medication, and blood tests every six months? And why was my body bigger when I was not overeating? I mean, sure, I may have eaten junk food, but not enough for my body to look less "slim" compared to everyone else.

It's hard to love our bodies when we have grown up being told "to eat less stodge," "tuck your stomach in," and that if we "continue to eat the way you do, you'll be obese"...And even as I was in my teens and then early twenties, my father never once attributed my weight to my medical condition; he would insist it was what I ate, and that I needed to eat less of whatever it was.

My point is, I read a quote from that specific September Letter and felt it was rather beautiful in its simplicity. In essence, why should we hate and belittle our own body when we love and appreciate those of our parents and ancestors before us? The people who have passed their body (genes, shapes, and everything that comes with it) down to us...and said body that we might then pass onto our children and grandchildren after us, who we will love and adore regardless.

I'm trying to be better, and although my decision to change my body was initially because I was told that I needed to, I refuse to let that continue to be the reason. Now, it is ultimately for myself and my own happiness so that one day I can be proud of myself and learn to love my body the way I was always supposed to.

I just wish I had had that hand to hold mine at the times I felt "disgusted" with my body, and that voice to tell me that I was beautiful just the way I was. So that's what I'm doing here for others. Telling you that you are beautiful the way you are, and that if you wish to change, you do so because YOU want to, not because someone else asks you to.

—Anonymous

I love this letter so much ♥ -B

What Is "Normal," Really?

with Dr. Naomi Torres-Mackie

*PhD, Licensed Clinical Psychologist
and Head of Research at the MHC*

NAOMI TORRES-MACKIE, PHD, *is a licensed psychologist, educator, and writer. She is also the head of research at The Mental Health Coalition, a partner organization to September Letters. The work that Dr. Torres-Mackie and her team do is cutting edge and empathetic—a rare intersection for which we are so grateful.* **xx Jaspre and Britt**

BRITT AND JASPRE: The Mental Health Coalition logo is a square peg in a round hole, which represents the idea that there is no normal. We love that. How does rejecting the idea of "normal" impact our lives?

DR. NAOMI TORRES-MACKIE: What is "normal," if you really think about it? At The Mental Health Coalition, we believe that there really is no normal. This idea allows for freedom from the stifling standards and expectations that we're all used to living with and that negatively impact our well-being. The concept of "normal" is essentially a box. But because no single box exists that fits everyone, the expectation to fit into the "normal box" leaves most people feeling like they're not good enough or there's something wrong with them. We're here to challenge the idea that there's a certain mold into which we should fit ourselves.

Much of the stigma surrounding mental health has to do with the shame of not fitting in. But if we celebrate being a square peg in a round hole, then experiencing mental health difficulties becomes just another life experience—not one to be shamed or looked down upon. By alleviating this stigma, we also alleviate negative judgments and self-appraisals that stand in the way of thriving.

BRITT AND JASPRE: Let's talk about thriving. How can we honor our true feelings when it feels unsafe or scary to do so?

NAOMI: The first step here is to assess the situation and determine if it is unsafe or scary. When it's unsafe, because safety really does come first, it's best to simply do what you need to do to get through it. In this case, you can practice acceptance of the situation you are in while looking for safe opportunities to change it.

Conversely, when a situation is safe but scary, taking the risk to be open about your true feelings is more about vulnerability, and it's time to go for it. We know from research on phobias and exposure therapy that the more you do something difficult like challenging yourself to honor your true feelings, the easier it becomes. That means that you'll be able to express yourself more freely, which cultivates mental well-being. Something we could all use more of.

SOME TIPS THAT CAN HELP YOU OVERCOME DISCOMFORT AND EXPRESS
YOURSELF INCLUDE:

....

1. **SEEKING OUT A TRUSTED EAR.** (Find someone you feel comfortable being vulnerable with and let the sharing begin.)

2. **ACKNOWLEDGE WHAT'S BEEN BLOCKING YOU** to honor your true feelings and think of clear, measurable steps you can take to remove those.

3. **PRACTICE TUNING IN TO YOURSELF.** This comes from cognitive behavioral therapy methods and involves setting a recurring time like the top of every hour to check in with yourself and ask, "What am I thinking, feeling, and doing right now?" Over time, it will become easier to both recognize and acknowledge your own internal emotional world.

BRITT AND JASPRE: How does writing play a role in therapeutic practice?

NAOMI: Writing aids with the process of externalization—of distancing yourself from the painful thoughts and feelings that can feel like they're part of you. When you put something down on paper it allows you to see it more clearly. Imagine holding a post-card of the Eiffel Tower up to your face so close that it touches your nose. It would be completely blurry. Now imagine moving it a bit farther away from your nose. The distance would allow you to see the image with more clarity. The same goes for letting thoughts swirl around in your mind versus writing them out. Once you externalize them, they feel less overwhelming and in seeing them clearly, you have a better chance of changing them.

BRITT AND JASPRE: And how can letter-writing be a tool for building compassion and empathy?

NAOMI: Letters are created to be shared, and sharing experience often allows individuals to see themselves reflected in others' experiences, even if those experiences are vastly different on the surface. One key to mental health is connection. Another is a sense of belonging. Sharing life experiences via letter-writing can help provide a sense of both. It's hard to not feel empathy for someone when you learn their story. A process of humanization and empathizing unfolds.

WE HAVE ALL FELT
LIKE A SQUARE PEG
IN A ROUND HOLE.
— KENNETH COLE

THE MENTAL HEALTH COALITION

Kenneth Cole, founder and chairman,
The Mental Health Coalition

From a young age we're taught we need to be something; we are supposed to make something of ourselves and our priorities go right into that. We go to college, we have to succeed, we have to get great grades and we have to get a great job... but no one ever tells us that we have to prioritize our health, and without our health few of those things are possible.

When I was in the hospital bed after my brain surgery, I saw things so differently. I realized I wasn't living in congruence with who I was and what I wanted. I had become this workaholic, which I realized was due to much of the programming from my youth. I also felt this odd kind of shame from my success due to the fact that I was making so much more money than my parents ever dreamed of in a far, far more glamorous profession. Who was I to work less or complain in any way, shape, or form?

So now I remind myself, and I remind every other woman out there, to listen to our bodies first. When we are in pain, suffering, or even just completely exhausted, we need to take the time to tend to ourselves. Health must be a priority, and not just physical health. Mental health, emotional health, and spiritual health matter just as much.

Our health is our wealth. This is my main message, which I will continue to share as long as I'm here.

xoxo Maria Menounos

Maria Menounos, New York Times *bestselling author and host of the digital series* Heal Squad

" Writing allows us to learn how to trust ourselves."

—ALEX ELLE

CHAPTER THREE

Courage + Strength

___

I was raised as a total free spirit. My parents taught me to dream the biggest dreams and then reach further. I had a pretty magical childhood, except for my health.

My surgeries started at two years old. I had strep so often that it was decided that my tonsils needed to be removed. I later learned that my sinus system didn't work properly and that when I got an infection my ears couldn't drain. I was allergic to everything. I spent days of my childhood at specialists' offices and in emergency and operating rooms. I would lose my hearing periodically. It would just go out. I burst my eardrums (not something I recommend) multiple times in each ear.

It affected my life more than I even realized at the time. Doctors told me things I didn't want to hear. My social life was altered. Basically, water, wind, or extreme sound wreaked havoc for my ears. I began to have anxiety and panic attacks every time I walked into a hospital or doctor's office. I was the kid who, at two years old, ran away from a blood draw and had my parents and three nurses in pursuit.

This cycle of surgeries and hospitalizations lasted well into my adulthood. I was at a loss. My mental health declined and my anxiety rose. One day, a friend suggested I see Ana Tucker, a hypnotherapist. She said she would help with my anxieties and despondence that had accumulated over the years. I was convinced Ana couldn't help and wasn't thrilled with the concept of someone going into my mind. I kept her number on my desk for years. My friend continued to urge me to reach out. Until one day, after another bout of illness, I hit my breaking point and made an appointment.

Unbelievably, Ana profoundly changed my life in one session. She helped me find my spirit and helped me get back in control of my body. After working with Ana, I was able to visit specialists and have my blood drawn without having panic attacks. It was a relief to finally acquire a tool that could help me. It inspired me to heal my body. I changed my diet, learned Transcendental Meditation, and began taking supplements. It turns out that for me a mix of hypnotherapy and a specific way of eating was key to my healing.

This has shown me one truth: When you feel different or you don't belong, that can be one of the greatest gifts. I have found that people don't always understand what they themselves have not experienced. Miraculously, my hearing returned to full power. All those experiences helped me be more empathetic to others' pain and fear.

Dear September, if you are suffering, feeling isolated, different, or lost, I hope you hold on to hope. Know that each day is a reset. No matter how many times you get knocked down, you can and you will stand up. I was told a lot of things about my health, but I never gave up on myself. I will not give up on you either.

Sending strength in what you seek.

Jaspre

Dear September

Change is hard. We like routine and familiar faces and objects. You like your coffee a certain way from that same coffee shop you pass on your morning commute to work. But today coffee wasn't an option, so you chose tea instead. You took your first sip. It wasn't your usual coffee. But it wasn't bad—the last time you had tea was with your best friend, who you love, so you thought of her and smiled and hoped she was doing well.

Yesterday you longed for a moment of summer as you put your winter coat on in the doorway. But the crunch of the autumnal leaves under your feet made you feel calm and suddenly you remembered how you used to run through them as a kid. So, for old time's sake, you ran through the leaves just one more time.

On Sunday you put your hand in your pocket for warmth and found a note from an ex-lover no longer with you, so you stopped to read it whilst replaying the fondest, sweetest moments in your head. All but a bittersweet moment, but you felt contented.

You see, my dear, what I'm trying to say is, change is of course a terrifying thing. But what makes change easier is that there is familiarity in everything we do. In everything we see. There is no need to be afraid. Change is merely a new direction to share with your favorite memories.

From, Annie

To my younger self,

You're valid. Everything you feel right now, the confusion, the discomfort in your own body, the emotions and thoughts that flood your brain. All of it is valid and has an explanation.

You're queer and nonbinary and your name is Raven.

For a while you will despise who you are and you'll lay in bed every night, praying to a god you're not sure you believe in to take away this part of yourself that is so new and scary.

But you'll learn to accept yourself for who you are, finding a community online. People like you who will understand you and your struggle.

Day after day you'll grow stronger and more confident in your identity to the point where you'll start your coming-out journey by telling your friends and your mum. Every single one of them will take the news very well and will welcome you with open arms.

It will be scary, and it will cause you the cold sweats every time, but it will be worth it because every single time you'll feel lighter and lighter, free from the chains of doubt and fear.

You will realize that your transness and queerness are the best things that ever happened to you, and they make you unique and special.

And it's beautiful, the way you'll be able to embrace and express yourself in a way that is true to you.

You'll be okay. Hell, you'll be more than okay. You'll thrive and I'm proud of you, proud of us and how far we've come.

Here's a lyric I wish I had found sooner because it will really help you navigate your gender identity and be happy with yourself:

"You're starting your life
From this moment now
Bird you can fly
Bird you can fly
You're breaking out
Out of your shell today." —Eyemèr, singer-songwriter

—Anonymous

I would tell my younger self it gets
worse, but it does eventually get better.

Anxiety and depression don't run your
life and you are stronger than you think.

Even though you may feel weak at times,
and like all hope is lost, you will survive.

Darkness is only for a moment.

You will see the light,

Scott

Scott Mescudi, aka Kid Cudi, musician,
actor, producer, writer, and activist

Dear fourteen-year-old self,

It's your twenty-eight-year-old self, here to say hello!

You're about to enter high school with your best friends. You're excited for your classes and extracurriculars—the world is your oyster. But I know there's one thing that is holding you back—or at least it feels like it does. It's something that you try to hide and ignore every day. Maybe when you get to high school it'll be better. Surely it'll be better in college, right? There's absolutely no way it won't be better by the time you graduate from college, because what adult stutters? You don't know any. Surely this is only a fourteen-year-old phase that you will outgrow in the next few years. I know what you're thinking: This won't, this can't be your life. (Spoiler alert: you're a twenty-eight-year-old who stutters.)

I know that Mom and Dad (and basically the entire family) treat your stutter as the elephant in the room. No one wants to voice it, especially you. If you voice it, it's real. No one offers support or guidance. You notice awkward glances amongst the family every single time you block on a word. At one point, Mom will actually ask you, "Do you even know when you're stuttering?" HA! Mom will make an effort to point out and do a happy dance whenever you go through periods of being quite fluent and will make equal effort to point out when you are blocking on words more often (because something must be wrong!). I know that because of the lack of support, you feel that you have to suppress your stutter. You avoid talking if you don't have to, you find substitute words and rephrase sentences...anything to not stutter. Anything to be fluent.

Overall, your stutter will not affect your friendship, or your dating life. (You're currently in a five-year relationship!) People will want to hang out with you. You will make new friends in high school, college, and after. They won't be embarrassed to be your friend.

It won't all be easy sailing, though. The first time you will be openly made fun of is in high school during your senior year in English Literature. The assignment is to pick a poem, any poem of a certain length, and recite it by memory in front of the class (our version of hell). Points will be taken off for mistakes. A boy will raise his hand and ask if that includes stuttering. (Since you've gotten so good at hiding your stutter and it is early on in the year, the teacher does not yet know you're a person who stutters.) The teacher says, "Possibly." Then the boy yells, "Sucks to be you [eighteen-year-old self]!" The entire class will laugh. Not one person will not laugh. Not one person will stand up for you. He'll only apologize and the laughing will quiet down after you start quietly crying at your desk.

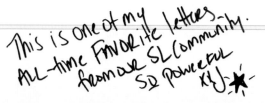
This is one of my
All-time FAVORite letters.
from our SL community.
SD Powerful
KJ

In college you will decide to do speech therapy. Mom is excited until she learns that it's not designed to "cure" your stutter, rather it's designed to help with confidence, moving out of your comfort zone, and learning techniques to help when you block on a word. Unfortunately, the copay per visit becomes too expensive and you're forced to quit.

During your time in speech therapy, you'll learn that people don't care about your stuttering as much as you think they do (though you still haven't quite embraced this idea yet). You'll also "disclose" for the first time. Yes, unfortunately it takes about twenty years, but you eventually say the words out loud to another human being who isn't a speech therapist: "I'm a person who stutters." It's a pretty big moment, yet so simple (and slightly anticlimactic).

Throughout college and after, there will be times during presentations or normal conversations where people will think you're nervous. You'll be afraid you appear unprofessional or unknowledgeable. Several people will point it out ("Wow you had some trouble there!"), but a lot of people will be understanding and patient. Many friends will have good intentions by finishing sentences or words for you instead of letting you speak a full thought yourself like a damn adult.

Over time, you will get more comfortable with your speech, but you still aren't exactly confident yet. Mom and Dad will still make your stutter the elephant in the room, so you continue to stutter at home and in social situations.

You won't officially disclose your stutter again until you're me—your twenty-eight-year-old self—to your boyfriend. Yes! It will take nearly five years to be confident enough to bring the subject up to your own boyfriend. It's not because you don't love him or don't trust him; it's still hard for you to say the words "I'm a person who stutters" out loud. When you voice it, it makes it real. (Side note: years ago, you told Mom that you were planning on disclosing to him. Instead of offering support, she said, "But don't you think he already knows?" I don't think she understood disclosing meant owning it yourself, voicing it, and no longer making it the elephant in the room.) If I could change one thing for you, it would be that you disclosed sooner and more often.

Unfortunately, even at twenty-eight, part of me is still holding out hope...maybe by thirty or forty I'll be completely fluent. Maybe by then my stutter will magically disappear.

On the days it's really hard and the nights you cry yourself to sleep, when it becomes days on end where you're afraid you'll never be able to say a complete sentence without stuttering, remember it's okay. This is you, me, us—and it's okay. It's okay to be a person who stutters. You are not any less of a person. You are not less knowledgeable or capable just because you can't always get a sentence out the way you'd prefer. It's okay. This is a beautiful life and you have so much to offer the world.

—Anonymous

What are you grateful for?

I am so grateful for nature. Enjoying the "simple things" in life, like the beauty of my home in the Pacific Northwest, can feel difficult when I am struggling with my mental health. But over the last year, just being in nature has been really grounding for me (once I stopped expecting it to erase all of my problems and uncomfortable feelings). Nature helps me feel more connected to reality and to myself.

Who would you like to thank and why?

I want to climb the world's highest peak and scream "Thank you, <u>Mom</u>!" She has helped me through every period in my life with love, patience, and grace as a badass single mom. I wish everyone had someone in their life like her. I love you, mama.

From, Lily Cornell Silver

Lily Cornell Silver, activist and musician

The strongest thing I've ever done for myself isn't an isolated act or event. It's a daily practice. The strongest thing I do is draw boundaries when they are needed. As a Latin woman growing up in the nineties, I was always a people pleaser. I said "yes!" to commitments, etc., before really asking myself whether or not I wanted to wholeheartedly participate in whatever I committed to.

I now try my best to pause before reacting. I evaluate how I feel about saying yes or no; not how it will be received. I take my power back.

Jordana Brewster

Why Author Anna Quindlen Believes Writing Will Save Us All

by Anna Quindlen

Novelist and journalist whose work has appeared on fiction, nonfiction, and self-help bestseller lists.

PULITZER PRIZE-WINNING ANNA QUINDLEN *has informed and captivated humanity with her words for five decades. A lauded journalist and author, Quindlen began her career at the* New York Post *before landing a role at the* New York Times, *where she gained a following for her columns. In the mid-1990s, Quindlen began to write novels, the facet of her career for which she is most widely known today. In her most recent book,* Write for Your Life, *she flips her perspective onto writing itself. Putting pen to paper, Quindlen believes, is an act that needs to be explored by every one of us. Writing is how we share, explore, discover, and document. And it is a means of saving us all. Here she shares with September Letters some of her sentiments around the very act that has served her and her readers all this time.*

THE THERAPY OF WRITING . . .

My research has shown that a variety of professionals, from doctors to therapists, are convinced that writing lessens stress and anxiety. I've encountered many anecdotes about this. When Sian Beilock, the president of Barnard College, and I were doing an interview, she told me about a study she'd conducted where they divided a group of students who were anxious about a math test into two groups: One group went off and studied for the test. The other group was asked to write about what they were feeling and why they were anxious about the test. The group who wrote about it did better on the test. This knocked my socks off because I thought, "There you go. There's the proof."

There's something about taking the time to think about what you're feeling and then putting it on the computer or paper in a discursive, slow, thoughtful way. This shows you the power of what you're going through and lessens the anxiety. It's magical.

THE POWER OF GOING DEEP . . .

The problem with so much of our communication nowadays, either in text or in emails, is that it's knee-jerk. It's not even really writing; it's more like free association. When we take time to go deep, we let what is inside of us out, not in a hair-trigger way, but in a thoughtful way.

THE BEAUTY OF EXAMINATION . . .

I've always written professionally. But I am a Catholic. I was raised in the Church, where there is something called examining your conscience before confession. My writing has forced me to examine my conscience. Over and over, I've written down something in a glib and thoughtless way that seemed clever or interesting. And when I've been faced with reading it over, it's forced me to go deeper and to be more authentic about who I am and what I care about. That's invaluable to me.

THE TRANSCENDENCE OF THE LETTER . . .

How many of us have wanted to have a serious or significant conversation with someone we care about and have done it either face to face or on the telephone and that night lay in bed thinking, "What did I say? Did it come across the way I meant it? Did I say what I was feeling?" Letter-writing is a version of speaking extemporaneously. Most gifted speakers speak with a text in front of them, which they have labored over. A letter is an emotional version of that kind of text. It's deciding what you want to talk about with someone you love and then taking time and care to go over it.

> WHEN WE TAKE TIME TO GO DEEP, WE LET WHAT IS INSIDE OF US OUT, NOT IN A HAIR-TRIGGER WAY, BUT IN A THOUGHTFUL WAY.

We sometimes fail to feel connected to other people because we've let these technologies, which are fast and dirty and glib, take over our communications. Sometimes letter-writing can make all the difference in terms of how we connect with the people we love and also how that connection can prevail over the years. People circle back to a letter in a way that is impossible to do with a phone call. With a letter, we remember when we sent or received it and it still feels so important and so good. It's significant that whenever we think about people saving letters, we think of them tied up with a ribbon.

This is so true! —B

They're a gift.

A ONE-WAY TICKET

Remember the ads that used to play on the radio asking, "Is your kid the next Disney or Nickelodeon star?" Well, I do. And I'm sure my parents remember them, too. I would always squeal from the backseat of my mom's gold Toyota Camry, "Me, me, me! I'm the next one! Can I go?! Please, please, please?!" Even at nine, I knew I had to move to Hollywood (or to Orlando... it was a thing back then) to really do what I love: entertain people.

While I knew I loved it, I didn't really think I could do it. I come from a very close-knit Cuban family. I'm a first-generation kid. Every decision I make is weighed against the sacrifices my parents and grandparents made. So trying to become the next . . . anything in show business was too much of a gamble.

Plus, if I left Miami, the only city I'd ever known, I'd be abandoning my family. I wouldn't be around to help my dad put up the Christmas lights in ninety-degree heat. My mom would probably revert back to the stone ages, never knowing how to update to any new technology. And what about my brother? My aunts? My cousins? Surely they all need me, too, right?

And then it happened. One day, as I was heading back home from my part-time job as a file clerk at a law firm, I realized I had to go. I had to be the next...ME! I had to find the strength to put myself first. I had to love myself enough to give my dreams a chance. To be my own person, to leave my comfort zone.

So I bought a one-way ticket to Hollywood (Orlando wasn't a thing anymore). This difficult, life-changing decision eventually showed me how strong my family bond is. How distance is no match to our love. How in pursuing my dreams, I'm actually doing exactly what my grandparents wanted me to do when they fled Cuba in 1967. I see the joy that comes from loving and believing in yourself. And that? That's the next level.

Chrissie

Dear September

Let them help you.

It is hard to ask for help, I know,
but it is the best thing you can do.

Always remember this time will
make you stronger.

From, Leonie

Letters From Friends

**AK Positive Thought
of the Day!**

**"MAKE YOURSELF AS
BIG AS YOU CAN!"**

—Amanda Kloots

Amanda Kloots, New York Times
bestselling author and cohost of The Talk

The Catharsis of Writing to Your Emotions

by Alex Elle

Author, Restorative Writing Teacher, and Certified Breathwork Coach

Writing allows us to trust ourselves.

I practice self-care by writing letters to myself. I teach folks how to write letters to their emotions, to root deeper into them or part ways with them—all with love and care.

I love sending a note card, a thank you card, or a care package with a letter in it to people. But when it comes to my mental health, healing, and self-care practice, writing letters to myself and to my emotions has been so cathartic. This reminds me to stand in my power, especially as I am someone who did not feel they had that opportunity growing up. In my adult life, I nurture my inner child, own my voice, own my stories, and connect with others—all by way of writing.

Whenever I'm in a rut, feeling bad about myself or about my work or so on, I will write a letter to the emotion or the feeling that's coming up. I'll get curious about why it's there. Then I give myself permission to let it go on the page.

It doesn't have to be super deep.

It can just be this release.

It can simply be permission to let go.

REMEMBER *You know what you need. You are your own greatest teacher. You may not feel that way today, but after you read that letter in six months, you will see that you knew what you needed . . .*

Such a good idea!

This.)

1. **TAKE A FEW DEEP BREATHS.** Writing a letter to your emotions and feelings can be triggering. Facing ourselves and our feelings on the page is hard. So breathe into this first.

2. **WRITE WITHOUT ANY JUDGMENT OF YOURSELF.** You're coming to the page with self-compassion in one hand and nonjudgment in the other. Sit down and allow yourself to be who you are and feel how you feel on the page without shame, without guilt, without judgment, and without harshness.

3. **SEAL THE LETTER.** This way you can read it later if you want to. I set a calendar reminder to open the letter in six months, or whenever it feels right.

So write the letter, seal the letter, and then, one day, read it.

Okay . . . I'm just gonna say it . . . So, here goes . . .

I once was in an abusive and very toxic relationship. I wasn't perfect. I got angry and said mean things. . . . But I know I didn't deserve what happened to me. And I think about it every day. And I don't think he does. I would actually bet money that he doesn't think about it. Even though I have recurring flashbacks of the intense, abusive moments almost every single day.

I didn't see a way out for a while. I was caught up in the cycle of apologies and forgiveness. I wanted to be able to love him. But the relentless verbal assaults were exhausting. So much so that I would be driven to collapse into bed for hours with no words left to give to my own voice because all I could hear was the barrage of his words that echoed loud and bounced back and forth relentlessly across the lonely rooms of my own head and heart. I became paralyzed. And looking back, I can see that was his way of manipulation and control. Then, the moments of public humiliation, and then the physical assaults, being chased, locked out of my own home while crying on the phone to my father for help, being pushed, pinned to the bed, and screamed at, having my phone taken and held hostage, screamed at so loud to get out of a moving vehicle that my eardrum burst, being told no one would ever love me if I left him, became too frequent to withstand. Deep down, I knew I was worth more, despite him drilling into me the exact opposite.

I was lost. But I started to listen. To myself. To my inner, most courageous, and vulnerable self. And I told Me to run . . . run as fast and as far away as possible. I knew that even though I was scared to be alone and scared of what people would think of me, I had to be free to find a better life. That this was not living.

My advice to you reading this letter is to trust your gut and believe in your worth as a beautiful human being. No one deserves abuse and there are others out there who can help you to get out. I'm thankful to say that I'm finding happiness now and this letter is only a glimmer of what I experienced. But I want you to know that you are not alone, and that if I can leave with my head held high, so can you . . .

Letters From Friends

xo Anna Camp

Anna Camp, actress and producer

Hey.

I know you're going through a lot. I don't even
have to know what's going on or where you are in
life to know that sentence is true. Because we're
always going through a lot. It's a lot to be a
person. It's a lot to be a woman. It's a lot.

I know what you're doing. Not like, right in this
exact moment in the future when you read this,
but generally. I know that you're pushing through.
I know that you're taking on more than you should
and putting yourself last. I know that late at
night, when everything is quiet, your mind spins
into shadowy corners, recalling your darkest
moments. I know that you're anxious and depressed,
but I also know that you're a warrior who loves
intensely and with her whole heart. You're so many
things. And you love being so many things. But
it's also fucking exhausting.

I'm just here to remind you that it's okay. Is
that some profound piece of wisdom? No. But
I think sometimes it's not about a specific piece
of advice that's going to unlock some deep,
philosophical question you've been trying to
answer. Sometimes it's just nice to remember...
it's okay.

You got through today.

You'll get through tomorrow.

                                   —Jenn

Jennifer Kaytin Robinson, writer, director, and producer

"Grief is not a problem to be solved; it's an experience of life.**"**

—DAVID KESSLER

CHAPTER FOUR

Love + Loss

You are a human.

Not an addict, or an alcoholic, or any of the worst things you've ever done. Addiction is an experience, one of many that can shape a life. It's not unique. It's not a flaw. It's not even that interesting. It's a natural human instinct—to soothe, to connect, to experience ourselves differently—gone awry.

—Laura McKowen,
We Are the Luckiest

This quote perfectly expressed a shift in opinion I've been trying to comprehend and put words to since my brother's death in July. This new perspective on addiction and alcoholism came after over twenty years of battling alongside in support of, and sometimes in anger toward, my brother Shane and his addictions. It also unfortunately came after he took his own life.

This is something I'll struggle with for the rest of my life. It's hard to not blame myself, especially since Shane lived with my daughter and me at the time of his death. I also know I tried to do everything I could to help him, and thinking of the what-ifs is a dangerous path to head down. Something else I'm certain of—Shane didn't do this because he didn't feel loved; he was just so, so tired.

Shane with his sisters, Ashleigh and Sonia.

There is a twelve-year age difference between Shane and me. I grew up worshipping the ground he walked on—he was my savior. He was also handsome, charming, funny, and loving. These are the things that defined my beautiful big brother as a person, not the mistakes he made. Those are the qualities I'll take with me forever.

You are NOT any of the worst things you've ever done. Read that again! You are not any of the worst things you've ever done. When someone makes a mistake, it's so easy to hold on to the visceral emotions—anger, self-pity, sadness, PRIDE. These emotions come easily because they make us feel justified, but they're exhausting nonetheless. Humans must put effort into understanding, compassion, forgiveness, and unconditional love. We must plant the seed we want to nurture and grow—anger or love. Whichever we decide, those roots bury deep and grow into the biggest trees.

Shane with his mom, Tama.

It's so easy to hold tight to anger and hatred, and to let someone's mistakes define who they are to you. It's also an unfair perspective to have, because not only are you limiting yourself to insincere human interactions, you're ignoring the fact that others could do the same to you. One bad day could define who you are in someone else's story, but that one day doesn't define your entire life. There's so much more to us, as humans, than our faults and bad days.

Anyone can look at pictures and videos of Shane with my daughter, Lily, to know the man he was. Shane's charisma knew no bounds, and Lily fell easily in love with him, just like I did when I was little. My daughter is only two and I struggle with her experience of this loss. I honestly believe she loved him extra because she knew his time here was limited. She's too little to understand that she can't talk to him or play with him again. She talks about him constantly and says the sweetest things that let me know he's still with her. It's incredible how much she picks up on. Even if she doesn't understand the concept of death, she still knows to be sad.

Shane with his niece, Lily.

An important thing I've learned in my grief is how many lives just one person's life touches. We weave this web of community, love, friendship, and connection throughout our lives. These are the things that matter: nurturing relationships, having compassion when it's in short supply, understanding instead of judging, and loving when you'd rather fight. All these things take patience and accountability.

My dad once asked me if I knew the meaning of unconditional love. I was a teenager at the time, trying to come to terms with Shane's demons and asking myself why, if he loved me as much as he claimed, I wasn't enough to keep him sober. In response he said, "Loving someone unconditionally means regardless of the choices they make and the pain they cause, you love them anyway." Not necessarily that you make yourself suffer, but that you can still love someone and not like them, at that moment. It's taken years of work for me to get to a point where I could unconditionally love Shane. But I did it. I love him more than I could ever say, regardless of his choices. I've since realized loving Shane always came easily, I just had to make the conscious decision to not take his choices personally and to not allow those choices to dictate my feelings toward him.

Love is the greatest gift of all, and I'm lucky to love and to have been loved by Shane Michael for almost thirty years. I'll always remember my brother as my savior, as the man who loved my daughter like his own, and as a charismatic bright light. He will be with me forever.

Shane, I know we'll meet again one day, and until then, I'll be missing you.

—Anonymous

The Strongest Thing I've Done for Myself

by Hannah Bronfman

Activist, Author, Founder of HBFIT, and On-Camera Personality

After working with a fertility specialist for months, I got pregnant for the first time in December 2018. I was launching my book *Do What Feels Good* in mid-January and, at my first book event, I remember being so overcome with joy, I burst into tears greeting people. I thought to myself, these pregnancy hormones are really getting the best of me!

A few weeks later I went for my twelve-week scan just before another event. I had a strange feeling walking in, but I got undressed and into a gown, and put my legs up. There was a long pause. The doctor said, "I don't see a heartbeat anymore," followed by a heartbreaking silence. I didn't know what to do or say. All I knew was that I had to call my husband immediately. And that's when I said it out loud for the first time and it hit me, this baby was not going to make it.

I can't remember the conversation Brendan and I had in that fragile moment because I immediately disassociated and shifted my focus to the event starting in five hours. I didn't want to cancel on the people showing up to support me. I felt like this was a major moment in my career; it wasn't going to be taken away from me, not after losing this baby. I was grasping to control some part of the situation, so I made the decision to show up with a brave face and let the show go on. I would grieve and mourn later.

The moderator greeted me when I arrived. As we caught up, she told me she was expecting a baby herself. I thought I was going to throw up. Struggling with fertility comes with so much jealousy and sadness. I can't describe the pain and disappointment I was feeling in that moment, but I had to find joy and happiness for her, too, even though I was beyond crushed on the inside. Once again, I dug deep, grabbed my strength tightly, and clenched my teeth hard while saying congratulations.

Later that night I had dinner with friends and told them what happened. They couldn't believe I hadn't canceled the event and, in that moment, neither could I. I was happy it had been a success, but I realized I had played into hustle culture and yielded to the pressure to prove my work ethic. I had prioritized work over my mental health, and as I sit here reflecting on that day, I wonder: would the "stronger" thing have been to cancel the damn event, sit on my couch, and feel all my feelings?

In my family, we have handwritten letters that have been passed down over the generations, and when we read them suddenly we feel you are in the same room together. Their character comes alive, whereas without the benefit of a letter you are looking at a photograph and imagining what they must have been like.

One of my most cherished letters is the one that my grandfather wrote to my grandmother before they were married, when he was eighteen. There are a few very romantic but reserved sentences such as "I hope you think of me once in a while..." Not demanding, but gentle and receptive.

The expression "the Art of letter-writing" is accurate. It's a skill, one that needs honing to master. I think that writing a letter is much more intimate, more revealing, more vulnerable. Because you are writing without knowing how your words are being received. When we are speaking, we look for feedback—if a person laughs, if they look interested—and then we pivot from there...With a letter, you have to wholly commit to the words you are writing down.

Beth

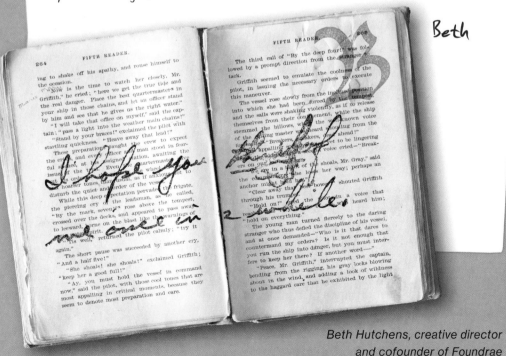

Beth Hutchens, creative director
and cofounder of Foundrae

Love, Loss, and Writing to Understand Our Grief

with David Kessler

Author, Public Speaker, and Grief Expert

WOW! A simple truth that holds incredible POWER —

This ↓

"If the love is real, the grief is real."

> **GRIEF IS ONE OF THE HARDEST REALITIES OF LIFE.** *It is also one of the most profound opportunities for growth. It was an honor to sit and talk with David Kessler, a leading grief and loss expert. Kessler has dedicated his career to understanding grief after his own experiences with loss, including the death of his mother when he was a boy, his youngest son, and recently his family dog. Kessler believes that grief shows us that we have loved and can be a beautiful reminder of the light in the darkness. We bonded over the shared grief of losing a beloved family pet. Kessler helps people explore their grief and understand that there is no one way to do it. It's personal, beautiful, and a part of life. We dive into it all here.* **x Jaspre**

JASPRE: You've written several books. How is the writing process important, both for you and for grief?

DAVID: What really got me, when I was in my thirties, was when I put my story on paper. My mother died when I was a child. And while she was dying in the hospital, there was a shooting, which I'd witnessed. I remember my father didn't want to talk about grief. So I became someone with abandonment issues, and I carried judgment for my father for not "doing grief" well.

I had told my story so many times before I decided to put it on paper. There's something so powerful about putting your story on the page. I always talk about how it's so important to witness grief and to feel seen. Writing is a way that you can see your own pain and to witness yourself.

When I finally put my story on paper, I saw the abandonment. I saw the pain. I saw the judgment of my father. I saw it all in my story.

Writing is powerful because it lets you see your own grief and offers a new way into considering others.

Then I decided to do something, which I still do now with people at my retreats and workshops. I wrote my story from my father's perspective. I had to imagine what his story would be like if he was writing it. So I wrote his story, as a man whose wife is dying. Who has no money. Who's going to have to raise a child alone and doesn't know how to be a parent.

For the first time, when I wrote his story on paper, I went from having judgment to compassion for him. Then I wrote my mother's story. Something powerful hit me on the pages that I had never seen. It dawned on me that my mother didn't abandon me. My mother died.

Writing is powerful because it lets you see your own grief and offers a new way into considering others.

JASPRE: In your work, have you come across a particular story or letter that has stayed with you?

DAVID: There is a letter and it's the hardest letter I've seen. I came across it while I was writing my book. I had a chapter on suicide and death by suicide, so I wanted to look at suicide notes and letters. And there was this one. I remember, as I was going through them, I was thinking, "What am I looking for in the writing?" It's not like I was looking for a good suicide note, there's no such thing. But I came across this note. The way this person described what they were experiencing and feeling, they took me into their brain. It was just so powerful. It showed their mental illness and struggle, and their care for other people. That will always touch me.

JASPRE: **When you feel particularly deep in grief, what are some tools to help start the healing process?**

DAVID: The first thing is to know that we're not meant to be islands of grief. We all want our grief witnessed. There's research on mirroring neurons in babies. When the parent smiles, the baby smiles. I remind people we actually don't grow out of that. We want our life, our pain, and who we are to be witnessed. We have a need to be seen.

We live in a grief-illiterate world that tells us we need to do things within a certain time-frame. I tell people that grief is an organic process. There's a part of your soul, psyche, psychology, emotionality that knows how to do this. It's all the noise from the outside world that's confusing, which causes judgment to get in our way. People tell us we're doing it wrong. We're crying too much, we're not crying enough. We begin to think of grief as a problem to be solved. And grief is not a problem to be solved, it's an experience of life. Don't "should" on yourself. "I should be over this by now; I should be better." We don't understand how long grief lasts. When people ask me, "How long should I grieve?" And I respond, "How long will the person be dead? If they're going to be dead for a long time, you're going to grieve for a long time. But it's important to know it doesn't mean you'll always grieve with pain." There's no right way to do grief. The goal of grief work is to remember with more love than pain.

JASPRE: **So many people ask themselves, "Why did this happen and what does it really mean?"**

DAVID: People get confused and think there is no meaning in tragedy. There's no meaning in a pet's death. There's no meaning in something like COVID, or partner abuse, or the death of a family member. Of course there isn't. The meaning is what you make afterward. The meaning is in us. It's what we do.

And, my gosh, writing is a means to meaning. Our words, our experiences, become meaningful on paper. In Brittany's experience, she saw that firsthand. Those words that were meaningful to her were meaningful to others. One of the things I learned from my first book is that writing is a reciprocal relationship. I can be up at 3 a.m. and write a sentence and burst into tears. Five years later someone in another country I've never met can tell me they were up reading that sentence and they burst into tears. There's something about our emotions that live through the writing and flow into one another.

Finding Healing in Her Own Words

by Hayley Kiyoko

Singer, Songwriter, Director, and Actress

"It's about watering the seed of self-love."

Sharing our stories helps people heal. Through my experience of sharing my vulnerability around my sexuality and my mental health, I was able to find a community that felt exactly the way I felt. This community made me feel like I wasn't alone—and it's been a huge part of my journey.

The more vulnerable we can be, the more accepting we become of ourselves and the more open we are to seeing that we aren't alone in our dark times and hardships. So many of us are going through the same things. ← agreed. so many ♥

HOW JOURNALING GIVES US STRENGTH

I am a songwriter, so journaling has always been a part of my process. It allows me to communicate and get in touch with myself. I've taken this even further when it comes to my journey with my mental health. I go through almost four journals a year. Even in those dark times, to be able to see your words and connect to yourself is so grounding.

ON NAVIGATING DEPRESSION

When you're battling depression, you may not have control a lot of the time. It can be so hard to change your mindset. What I've found is that when I journal, even though I may not be able to control my thoughts, I can keep pushing through this. Journaling has allowed me to continue to navigate what I'm going through each and every day. Through journaling, I've realized: Yes, this is hard. Yes, I don't know what's going to happen. Yes, I don't know what tomorrow will bring. But I do know that I'm going to keep going—and I'm not going to give up.

WHY WRITING IS A PORTAL TO UNDERSTANDING

When I open my journal and look at what I've written, I realize, wow. . . this is how I feel! It's amazing and empowering. It allows you to really see things. Then you start asking why. You open this dialogue and start peeling back these layers, and you keep asking more and more questions. Then, all of a sudden, you see that it's because of this insecurity or this fear or your inner child. You're able to discover and learn so much about yourself.

ON WHAT TO KNOW IF YOU'RE GOING THROUGH A HARD TIME

I want to offer you compassion and kindness and grace to feel the way you feel. Know that things are going to get better. Self-love is like a seed: the more you water it, the more it will grow. So this moment in time is about watering that seed of self-love so that it will blossom and grow.

xo Hayley

I grieve a mother who is still alive.

It can be easy to forgive and still love, but it's not always easy to forget and move on in a relationship with a loved one.

I feel guilty sometimes, like it's my fault. I fall into this black hole of, "I am a horrible daughter. What kind of daughter just cuts ties with her own mother?" Then I remember what kind of mother she often was. Sure, there were good moments and some happy memories, but they are blurred by a lot of sad ones.

I think what hurts the most is the loss of what could have been. Had she gotten help when I was younger, had she chosen stability, healthy relationships, or just accepted healthy boundaries, I think our relationship would look a lot different.

She was lost and hurting, this I know. She had her own demons and things to deal with. I tried to be understanding for years, but it consumed me. I was tired of taking care of her. I wanted to be a mother to my own children, not to her.

Now that I am a mother, I know. I know that she could have done it. She just didn't have the right support or resources to aid her along. I fight every day for a healthy mindset. I breathe, do yoga, exercise, eat healthy, go to counseling, surround myself with positive and supportive people. I never sugarcoat the pain, though. My kids see rawness. They know mommy has sadness sometimes, but that she works to be happy. They know that they are the kids, and I am the mommy. They know that they come first.

Not seeing her is the hardest thing I've ever done. I tell my children about her and how beautiful she is and how I love her.

This is the thing: Every relationship is different. It isn't black and white. My relationship with my mom was different from her relationship with my siblings. Family members didn't experience the same toxic behavior that I experienced as the child. I was the oldest. She confided in me. She relied on me financially. I remember the divorce. I remember all the late nights and early mornings she was away while I cared for my siblings.

This is my story. My pain. No one else can tell it for me.

I am not mad at anyone. Just sad for the loss. I grieve all the loss.

I hope she is cared for. I hope she feels love. I hope she has some kind of peace and will someday understand. I hope she doesn't hate me.

I did what was best for me and that's okay. Nothing is set in stone and every day is new. Who knows what tomorrow will bring? I will bring to it love and an open heart, knowing I am doing what is right for me in this moment in time.

One day at a time. One hurt at a time. I will get through this.

—Anonymous

Finding Your Flow State

by Jay Shetty

#1 New York Times Bestselling Author, Purpose Coach, Former Monk, Host of the #1 Health and Wellness Podcast On Purpose, and Chief Purpose Officer of Calm

I talk a lot about meditation, but I don't talk as much about flow states. The thing is, there are tons of ways we can experience flow. But it's a challenge for most of us because one of the prerequisites for flow states that most of us struggle with—which you probably know if you've ever meditated—is focus. I know from the questions I get, and from my own struggles to focus, that bringing our attention to one thing at a time is more challenging than ever these days.

One of the ways we can both achieve more flow states and get more focus is to routinely engage in an activity where we find flow easily. This would be something that requires all your attention so that your brain can create an immersive environment. It's usually something that's challenging, and it's something about which you're curious or passionate. For me, when I'm writing scripts or presentations—when I have to dig deep creatively—that's one place (aside from meditation) where I routinely get into flow. I turn off my phone. I make sure I have a decent block of time with no interruptions. And I go for it.

I struggled at first. This is normal. As our brains get ready for flow, they release neurochemicals and hormones designed to help us focus and learn, and those can feel agitating. The key is to stick with it. Struggle is the gateway to flow. You've probably experienced that before. Maybe you sat there and thought, "There's no way I can do this!" but you kept at it, and at some point, something clicked. The next thing you knew, hours had gone by, or the opposite—time expanded, and ten minutes felt like an hour. That's flow. And its effects on our brain are amazing. We get more a-ha! moments in flow because of the gamma waves we generate. We get chemicals and hormones that make us feel really good. And science shows that people who get into flow states regularly feel more of a sense of meaning and purpose in life.

So, if you want to feel better, and be more productive to boot, find your flow. It can be anywhere. Running. Reading. Dancing. Spending quality time with your kids. In fact, anything that feels playful can be a great source of flow. (Plus, research shows that our brains learn better when we're engaged in play.)

The good news is that once you start to hit flow states—any way you get them—more flow will follow. It will become easier. As the saying goes, "Flow begets flow." And when you start to feel more flow, you'll begin to feel better.

Grief is a strange thing. It hits you in so many different ways that I never thought were possible. People say there are five stages you go through when you lose a loved one, but I learned the hard way there are so many more.

In October, I lost my grandmother to colon cancer and a huge part of me felt lost as well. She is the woman who inspired me to be the person I am today. She raised me and taught me the true meaning of kindness and strength. We were two peas in a pod in every way. So, when I got the call that she had colon cancer and we would at least have some time left with her, I tried to prepare myself for that loss. What I didn't expect was for her to be gone a week later.

I went through the typical emotions of denial, anger, depression, and bargaining, but those were just the tip of the iceberg for me. My journey started with denial and anger. But that led into something so much harder to deal with: loneliness and emptiness. I felt like a huge part of me was missing. I felt like that feeling would never go away. My wife and friends were there and trying to understand the pain I was experiencing. But no matter how hard they tried, I still felt like an empty shell. It felt like the love I was given by so many in that moment couldn't equate to her love. So I closed myself off to nearly everyone and stayed in that shell.

Then guilt hit. That was a fun one. I felt guilty for being alive, for not helping her catch the cancer sooner, for having love from other people, for not being okay after a certain amount of time. Probably the biggest of all was feeling guilty about not being there for those grieving as well.

My journey with grieving has been one of the hardest and strongest times of my life. I went to therapy almost every other day and worked with my doctor on a medication routine. My own personal healing began when I started to accept help again.

I basically had to rediscover who I was without one of the most important people in my life. It was a path to self-discovery, in a way. My journey is by no means over. I have been battling the ups and downs nearly every day. But I have also started to accept that it will be okay.

I learned that time cannot be a measurement for your grief.

I am nearly three months in, and I can say with 100 percent certainty that I am not fully through the healing process. But every day is a new step in the right direction, and those tiny steps are powerful. And let me say this hasn't been a solo journey, as much as I initially thought it was.

My grandmother may not physically be here, but I know she is all around me. I know she taught me what strength is, and each day I am exhibiting that through my progress. And every day will be a constant reminder of just how lucky I was to have her in my life.

X Cynthia

The Transcendence of Love Found through Writing

with Jason B. Rosenthal

Public speaker and author of the memoir,
My Wife Said You May Want to Marry Me.

"You may want to marry my husband."

IT'S HARD TO WRITE ABOUT JASON ROSENTHAL *without tearing up. Jason was married to a beautiful woman named Amy, a prolific memoirist and author. In March 2017, the* New York Times *published an essay by Amy in its Modern Love column titled "You May Want to Marry My Husband." Amy, who was fighting ovarian cancer, wrote about how she wanted Jason, her husband of twenty-six years, to find love again after she was gone. Ten days after her article was published, Amy died. In the time since Jason has been a sounding and beautiful voice on grief and resilience. His book and talks (I cried watching his TED Talk) offer solace to all of us living with loss, grief, and isolation. This is a deeply emotional story that proves how writing, in all its forms, gives love a means to transcend.* **x Britt**

BRITT: Do you feel that writing is a part of something that still connects you and Amy?

JASON: In a way, it does. I don't ever put myself on the same level as Amy as a writer. That's what her passion was. She just lived to express herself with words and creativity, so I don't hold myself up to that incredible standard. But I like what you said because for sure we are connected by certain words, and when she wrote that essay that appeared in the Modern Love column, I had no idea what was going to happen to me and my life because of it. We didn't anticipate the incredible responses that we received because of that essay. That began my first foray into speaking about things that I've shared now with the world. I gave that TED Talk in April of the following year, after Amy died. That immediately resonated with people in such an incredible way that it motivated me to continue to speak that way, and then eventually to start to write that way as well.

BRITT: With the responses you receive, do you feel that people connect with your story?

JASON: Absolutely. That was much to my surprise, to be honest with you. What I've been writing repeatedly, and saying repeatedly, is that I've learned a lot through this process of losing my wife, but I also learned that loss is loss, and all of us, in some way or another, experience loss throughout our life. So when Amy's essay came out, and then I did my TED Talk, people flooded me with all kinds of stories of their own. It has been so beautiful and rewarding.

BRITT: We always think that we're going through this alone, and when someone speaks out, it gives permission for the next person to feel brave to do the same thing. I'm sure that's why you have received so many responses. I love that you have said we're all grieving and we're always grieving. What advice do you have for someone who is grieving a tremendous loss?

JASON: There are different phases of grief. There are the famous "stages of grief," which I'm not sure I subscribe to, but there's certainly the first year-ish where the intensity of that grief is so overwhelming and overpowering. There is not much you can do to get out of it, to be honest. So I tell people just to dig in there and take as much time as they need, especially following a very significant loss.

Then my advice is some wisdom I received early on, and that is to know, and this is my promise to you, that eventually you will have moments of joy, clarity, laughter, of happiness that you perhaps thought that you would never have again. Those things do resurface and it's important to lean into that when it happens. It's important to acknowledge that it's a process that comes and goes. And like you said, it's never going to go away. That would make it impossible for us to deal with something so meaningful, to say that it's not going to be a part of our life forever. Now, these years later, I can tell you with some hindsight that there are moments of joy and beauty and love.

BRITT: This is quite personal. Do you feel it was even more powerful that Amy wrote the letter for public consumption as opposed to just writing it to you? That spoke to me like it was healing for her to do.

JASON: Absolutely. She was such an incredibly prolific writer, but also, she was a hard worker. This was just stuff that was all inside of her and had to come out. She had this one final goal before she died, and that was to write this essay, to get it published, and she knew where and when and how she wanted it published. The reason that it spoke so powerfully to so many people all over the world was that it was brutally honest. It was sad as sad can be. But it was also funny and interesting.

Like I said before, I had no idea what this was going to do to my life, nor did I know that she wanted to write this for me. But I do think on many levels that she was aware it wouldn't just touch me, but that it would indeed touch many, many, many people and affect their lives in an incredibly positive way.

Sending Thousands upon Thousands of Letter "Hugs"

with Jodi Ann Bickley

Founder of One Million Lovely Letters Jodi Ann Bickley is the queen of letter-writing. We don't say this lightly. Through her project one million lovely letters, she has written more than six thousand letters to people across the world.

THIS ALL STARTED IN 2013. *Jodi was in the trenches of depression. She was bed-bound and planning to end her life, when she watched a silly little video online that made her laugh. "And I thought, if I can laugh now, in the midst of this, then maybe I can start to climb out," she tells me. So Jodi wrote messages on Facebook and Twitter telling the world: "If you're having a bad day or week or month, email me and I'll handwrite you a lovely letter and just a hug in an envelope." Jodi's been doing this ever since. It makes Britt and I cry with joy just thinking about it.* **x Jaspre**

JASPRE: Your story is so amazing. Is there a reason why you chose letter-writing to connect with people?

JODI: Well, letters have always been a big part of my life. My nan died when I was five, and my mom told me and my brother to write a little letter to heaven. So we wrote these little letters and told our nan about our day. I remember that feeling like enough. It gave us closure.

Growing up, I'd always leave notes for people on the bus or in books. I might have conversations with people in the back of science textbooks; people saying that they're having a bad day. I wouldn't be trying to fix them, because I'm not a therapist, but I offer a little comforting shoulder.

With One Million Lovely Letters, it's never been me saying "I'm going to fix you." I can't. But I realized I can be like a hand to hold in the storm.

↖ Beautiful

JASPRE: You put so much work and time into writing these letters. People have reached out to you to tell you how your letters have changed their life. Did you ever expect this reaction?

JODI: I didn't expect it at all. I used to always write my address on the back in case it got lost in the post. People would write me back to tell me what had happened since the letter.

One of my first letters was to a couple who had unfortunately lost a baby. The mother wrote to me asking if I would write a letter to the father because she was getting lots of support, but he wasn't. I wrote to him and later they sent me a reply saying that they were going to have another baby. When my book was released, the first photo I got on the day of release was a picture of their newborn baby.

I've got them all in boxes, loads of replies. It's all life stories of how a letter or an act of kindness, even a smile on the street, a flicker of human connection, can change everything. That's what the letters are. It's reminding lots of people that they're loved and not on their own.

JASPRE: Where do you see letter-writing going? We feel like it's an ancient modality coming back. What do you think?

JODI: People are craving it and are in desperate need of it, that connection and being seen. I'm always on my phone. But we're not looking up at each other and connecting on that level. That's what a letter is: It's investing time in someone and something. And getting a letter feels like a treasure. I'm not sure about you, but I still have all of my old boyfriends' letters, and all of my mum's letters from when I went to college. I've got everything still because it feels special. It feels like someone saw me. Someone noticed me. They took the time.

exactly ↑

> *It's all life stories of how a letter or an act of kindness, even a smile on the street, a flicker of human connection, can change everything. That's what the letters are.*

Hey you,

This is a little note to ask you to stay. I know that's the hardest thing you can possibly think of doing right now when everything is so loud and so much and it has been for a while. I'm not asking you to stay because it's going to remarkably get better, you and I both know that's not how it works, but the temporariness of it all is for sure. The raging lows like right now can swing into those incredible highs when everything feels like it could be out of a film, one of those really cheesy ones that make you cringe and feel the utmost joy in equal measure. It can equally swing into days when everything isn't wonderful and it's terrible but existing just doesn't feel as heavy and as painful as it does today and I promise you that it's coming, as sure as the tides roll in and out and the storms roll through this. I promise you— it will not stay this heavy forever. You are loved beyond measure, beyond anything that you'll allow yourself to believe right now—this is me shouting from the rooftops, a stereo outside your window, a billboard on your morning commute, every day, that never goes away. YOU ARE SO LOVED, for all that you are, for all of the heavy and all of the light, I am here for it always. Nothing is ever too much, you are never too much, however hard it gets, however dark the nights, the days, and all in between I am here with a torch, a raging fire, burning as bright as the you that you are struggling to see, I am here. I am here. I am here. You are never on your own. I've got your hand and we're gonna make it home.

All of my love,

Jodi

Jodi Ann Bickley

You are
loved
beyond
measure.

"As humans, one of our core needs is to be seen and to be connected to other humans."

—DR. POOJA LAKSHMIN, MD

CHAPTER FIVE

Fear + Anxiety

Dear September

Dear younger self,

The world is hard. It will toss you on the ground and leave you gasping for air. People are mean, and life isn't always fair. You will watch yourself struggle until you are sure that there's no hope.

I promise you. Do not give up. You will be tempted hundreds of times. You will do things you are not proud of. The world will tell you to give up and to give in.

But there is so much more to life than the bad. You will get a dog. You will have a boyfriend, your first kiss, and get married. You may not be sure what you want your future to look like right now, and that's okay. Just make sure you stick around for it.

I know my younger self won't actually get to read this. I know that these are regrets that I will have my whole life. But in writing this, I hope I can help somebody else. Give them hope in a future that seems so far away.

So whoever is reading this, stay. No matter what comes your way, do not give up.

—Anonymous

Storytelling Is the "Crux of Being Human"

by Harrison Miller

Engineering student, writer, and just a guy trying to help

In March 2022, Harrison Miller posted to his social media a letter he wrote announcing he was "medically retiring" from college football. Harrison was a star lineman. He had a perfect GPA. Legions of fans. But he was crumbling on the inside. In his open letter, he shared how he struggled with depression and suicidal ideation. He lamented over society's contrived views around mental illness. "This is not an issue reserved for the far and away," he wrote. "It is in our homes. It is in our conversations. It is in the people we love."

Harrison's vulnerability ignited a wave of support and relief. His letter-writing also proved the power in sharing one's story.

SO BRAVE!

ON THE MAGNITUDE OF THE WRITTEN WORD . . .

I wasn't planning to make my announcement in a letter format. But as I was going through my treatment, my sports psychologist encouraged me to write short stories to help me process my thoughts. I knew my message had to be concise so it could be shared clearly over social media. Posting screenshots of small fonts that were difficult to decipher would cause it to lose its shareability, its stickiness. That was a fun challenge to boil down my thoughts to the bare bones. So I never really intended to write in this format, but it was a great writing exercise to put my thoughts together this way and share them publicly.

FOR BRINGING PEOPLE TOGETHER . . .

The crux of being a human is storytelling and sharing stories. I've always been so astonished by the power of language. There are times when each of us has been on the bad side of misused language, of language that is wounding and biting. That's why I think it's beautiful to share language that is uplifting and honest. That cuts through the fat of everything. When I read a good book, it feels like eating a filling meal. It's so great when you can eat a story and you feel satisfied and filled afterward instead of feeling deprived.

FOR EMBOLDENING THE CONVERSATION AROUND MENTAL HEALTH . . .

These stories of mental health are so honest and truthful and heartfelt. It fills us with substance as opposed to being met with vapor when we close our mouths. If we're wishing to change what our attitudes are about mental health, or really any topic, writing and storytelling will be the impetus of that.

FOR TRANSCENDING DEATH AND TIME . . .

You share company with great writers. That's the beautiful thing about a book. It's as if you're at a coffee shop with them and they're speaking to you. That's the effect of reading great literature or great prose or poetry: It allows you to live a thousand lives in one. I've been able to read about an old New England whaleman. And I've been able to read about the Musketeers in France.

It's incredible that language and thoughts transcend thousands of years and can still be equally beautiful.

IF WE'RE WISHING TO CHANGE WHAT OUR ATTITUDES ARE ABOUT MENTAL HEALTH, OR REALLY ANY TOPIC, WRITING AND STORYTELLING WILL BE THE IMPETUS OF THAT.

Dear September

I'm going to say something that I have never said aloud before. Not even alone to myself, because I've been afraid.

I've been afraid of the judgment.

I've been afraid of other people's opinions.

I've been afraid of the reaction of my friends and family.

But I'm done being afraid.

I'm done living in denial.

I'm done being someone else than my true self.

I know now who I am.

I know now that it is okay to be myself.

I know now that I don't have to hide.

I know now that I am going to be okay.

So here it goes:

Hi, my name is Max and I am female to male transgender.

Max

you Max!

Three Ways to Care for Your Heart and Mind

by Dr. Pooja Lakshmin, MD

Psychiatrist and the Founder and CEO of Gemma

WE HAVE A LONG WAY TO GO *before mental health is not only respected, but paramount. This is Dr. Pooja Lakshmin's fight. A board-certified physician psychiatrist specializing in women's mental health, an entrepreneur, and author of the book* Real Self-Care: A Transformative Program for Redefining Wellness (Crystals, Cleanses, and Bubble Baths Not Included), *Dr. Lakshmin reminds us that society makes it hard to prioritize wellness. There are costs, repercussions, and stigmas. People, primarily women of color, are penalized for making choices to put their health first. Dr. Lakshmin calls this the "tyranny of self-care." But how can we still take the best possible care of our hearts and minds? Even if the system makes it hard, we can find our own ways to stay strong. We asked Dr. Lakshmin to share a few ways to do this through writing.* **xx Britt and Jaspre**

#1: JOT DOWN POSITIVE MOMENTS

Keep a list on your phone of times you felt good. "It doesn't necessarily have to be big accomplishments," says Dr. Lakshmin. These can be large events or small daily moments, such as when you went to the lake and felt peaceful. Keep it in your phone so it's accessible. That way when you have bad days you can be reminded of a period where you felt good, she says.

#2: KEEP A "HYPE FILE"

You know when someone tells you something positive about yourself? Record that, says Dr. Lakshmin. "This is feedback that you've gotten, whether it's professionally or whether it's from friends or family members." Make it easily accessible so that you can

This is something we put into practice immediately! x J

look at it and remind yourself that other people think you're doing good things. "And that helps! Of course, we shouldn't be basing our self-worth on the reflections of other people. But as human beings, we do need that positive affirmation, we do need that feedback, so it helps to have that handy when you need it."

#3: WRITE A LETTER — TO YOURSELF OR SOMEONE ELSE

"What's so painful about mental health conditions is that most folks go through them feeling largely invisible. When we write letters, we make the invisible visible. So whether you're the one writing the letter or whether you're the one reading the letter, to see those emotions—to see those experiences named—can make you feel seen in return."

"WHEN THINKING BACK ON THE BEST MOMENTS IN MY LIFE AND THE WORST MOMENTS IN MY LIFE, THE THING THAT HAS HELPED ME PROCESS AND HEAL FROM THOSE PERIODS OF TIME IS MAKING SENSE OF IT IN A STORY. IT'S BEEN ABOUT CREATING AND UNDERSTANDING THE NARRATIVE FOR MYSELF. I DO THAT THROUGH WRITING."

—DR. POOJA LAKSHMIN, MD

Dear September

I'm doing really great, Dad.

I've finally forced myself to talk to a doctor about my anxiety and depression. After the many years I pushed my mental health aside and tried to stay strong and battle it alone, I finally allowed myself to seek help. And that's okay, I'm glad I did. I got some medication that's really helping. For the first time in years, I've started feeling closer to my old self again. I smiled today, and it wasn't forced. I laughed today, and it wasn't to hide my cries for help. I got up today, and it wasn't because of personal obligations but because I was excited to go out into the world.

I'm doing really great, Dad.

—Anonymous

Anxiety creeps up on you slowly. It's constantly lingering around you waiting for the perfect imperfect moment to attack. Then, in an instant, it attacks. Suddenly, you can't catch your breath. Your 20/20 vision turns into looking at ten frames per second. Your voice becomes ten octaves higher to match the fast metronome tapping of your shoe. Every possible mistake you've ever made is rushing through your mind at once, pages and pages of . . .

Did I say thank you to the barista this morning? Damn, now she probably things I'm a b*tch. She's probably talking to her co-workers about how terrible I am, hopefully the people in line didn't think the same. I need to go back and leave a tip—I'm tired. I'm always tired. Maybe I should ask for less hours at work. No, I can't, then I won't have enough money for school, my car, my phone bill, my insurance; then I'll have to drop out, my car will get taken away, I'll be in debt, get a second job, disappoint my family—am I walking too fast? Oh, I'm walking too fast. Now that man is looking at me; he probably thinks I'm crazy. I'll just smile. I can't smile, then he'll think I'm flirting, then talk to me, then follow me, then—what am I thinking? I'm fat and ugly, why would he at all be interested in me? Everyone can tell these jeans are too tight. They're all judging me. I'm fat. I'm ugly. I'm fat. I'm ugly. I'm fat. I'm ugly. My heart is really racing, am I having a heart attack? F*ck. I think I'm gonna pass out. It's probably since I haven't slept in three days. I'll buy melatonin later. I take too much melatonin, is that bad? But I can't sleep without it. Am I addicted—that guy has been following me for three blocks. Shoot, he saw me look at him. Should I stop and let him pass? What if he's not following me? He'll think I'm weird. But where could he possibly be going? Four right turns, that's what my mom taught me. Hell, I'll just go into this store. Now I have to buy something; it's rude if I don't. I don't have any cash. Damn. I'll Apple Pay, do they take Apple Pay? I don't want to ask. Let me look for signs. Do I look suspicious? They probably think I'm steali—oh, this is so cute! It won't look good on me, though. Nothing looks good on me. I hate my body and yet I don't do anything to change it. I probably should, but I never do. I'm late for work! Go go go go. You're gonna get fired. You're fired. What am I gonna say? Just pay and leave. Did I say thank you?

Shit. I forgot to inhale.

Breathe. Just breathe.

You're fine. You're safe.

Allow your thoughts to pass you by. You'll be okay. You are so much stronger than you think you are.

xo Rosie

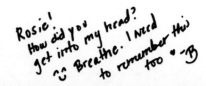

The Life-Enhancing Practice of Transcendental Meditation

with Bob Roth

Chief Executive Officer, David Lynch Foundation

"We are at war with trauma and stress."

WORDS CANNOT EXPRESS *the impact Bob Roth has had on my life, as well as on so many others' lives. One of the most revered meditation instructors, Bob has taught Transcendental Meditation (TM) to thousands of people across the globe for more than fifty years. He's also authored many books on the subject. Roth is grounded, kind, wise, and empathetic. During the height of the COVID-19 pandemic, I, along with countless others, joined his daily zoom to practice TM with Bob at 7 a.m. To be able to meditate with this icon was a privilege, and it felt important to be part of a large group of people meditating at once. His approach to our collective wellness is forthright. "We're in a pandemic of trauma," he tells me and Britt. "And there's never been a greater need for meditation."* **x Jaspre**

JASPRE: What impact does letter-writing have on you?

BOB: There's a lot of research on what letter-writing does. This means handwriting it out, not just typing it but handwriting it out. There is data about how this activates so many parts of the brain and integrates them. It's the transformation. It's not just a passing mental mood or emotional mood, but it's actually transforming the way your brain is functioning. I've heard people talking about the value of letter-writing more since COVID. It is a therapy that integrates your deepest emotions, in the privacy of your solitude. It's a very profound healing tool.

JASPRE: You were eighteen when you first started meditation. Why were you attracted to the practice?

BOB: I was the last guy in the world you would ever think was going to be a meditator. I was just between my freshman and sophomore years in college. This was the late sixties in the San Francisco Bay Area and the whole world was exploding. I had worked for Senator Bobby Kennedy, who was running for president. I became very socially aware that I wanted to create change. When he was assassinated, it was like an older brother or a favorite uncle—I can't even say. It was devastating.

I resolved that I wanted to become a lawyer and then a US senator so I could change the world by changing the laws to provide for equal access to life, liberty, and the pursuit of happiness for everyone. It became very clear to me in the first three months at college there that everything was so politically polarized. I realized that politics was never going to heal the soul of the nation. Politics is all about compromise, which is fine, but too much of it is about comprising the truth. I think politics is important, but for me, pursuing a life path that could uphold truth was the most important thing.

After Bobby Kennedy died, I was just left suspended. I didn't know what to do. I certainly didn't know of anything "inner." I was just trying to find a center. There was one guy who was working with me at Swensen's Ice Cream Parlor. He was just so steady. Turned out that he was doing something called Transcendental Meditation. I said, "I'll go in and after five minutes if I don't like it I'll just walk out." My experience was significant. Deep relaxation. One of my first thoughts afterward was that I wanted to teach kids to meditate. That was over fifty years ago. So now I run the David Lynch Foundation and we've taught over one million kids to meditate in the US and all over the world.

JASPRE: One thing that I love is there is no wrong way to practice TM. For someone interested in meditation, what would you say to them?

BOB: There's never been greater interest in meditation than there is today, for good reason. There have never been more opportunities to learn to meditate than there are today. And there's never been more confusion about what meditation is. Nobody knows what it is, they just go, "Oh, this magazine had five steps to become an expert meditator" or "here's an app where the person tells me to relax" or "it plays rain" or "there's the TM meditation where you get a mantra," but nobody actually knows. Despite the confusion, there's a real need for meditation. We are at war with trauma and stress. This is us fighting for life.

The way you eliminate confusion is you do some research. Look for data. Don't look for marketing and branding and buzzwords and endorsements. Look for solid data. Do your research and then try it. If it doesn't work and if it doesn't fit, if you find it difficult to do, try something else. I recommend Transcendental Meditation—but I recommend finding out for yourself.

JASPRE: As we know, TM is practiced in two twenty-minute sessions a day. What is the importance of practicing twice a day?

BOB: It's a tough world out there. It's coming at us faster and more furious than ever before. The US Surgeon General said, "If adults are swimming in an ocean of stress, our children are drowning in it." You want to start the day with as much resilience and with as much strength as you can. I say you meditate first thing in the morning to give you freedom, resilience, and strength, so that you can handle all that's coming at you, and then you do it at the end of the day to wash off the stress.

When you're hot and sweaty, you wouldn't just get into bed, or you wouldn't sit down to dinner. You'd take a shower. So wash off the stress of the day, enjoy your evening, and sleep better at night. That's the ideal.

BRITT: How does meditating change our brain chemistry?

BOB: It's the experience. Every experience distinctly changes the brain. If you listen to classical music, it has one effect on your brain. If you listen to heavy metal music, it has another. If you watch a romantic comedy, it has one effect on your brain. If you watch a horror film, it has another. During TM, if you close your eyes and you dive into the quieter levels of the ocean—your own quiet mind—you experience that deep settled-ness within. Even though it's not a flashy experience, it has a completely transformative effect on your brain. It creates what neuroscientists call a state of restful alertness, where your body is profoundly relaxed, but your mind is quiet and awake inside. So it's the experience in meditation that changes the brain.

But here's the second part. There's a term called neuroplasticity. This is like when you are a kid and you learn how to tie your shoe. You fumble around, fumble around, and finally, you got it. It's not that your fingers remember how to do it. It's those connections in the brain, it's called neuroplasticity, all those connections that happen, those moments you're learning to tie your shoes—they lock-in. And the more you practice, the better you get at it. That's your brain's neural pathways changing. So when you meditate twice a day, you have this profound experience in meditation. It carries over throughout the whole day. It's not that you're intellectually remembering to be calmer or more alert or more creative. You changed your brain in meditation. Your brain starts releasing dopamine, which is the happiness and pleasure center. It releases serotonin, which is that well-being chemical. The purpose of TM is not as an end in itself, but for life.

JASPRE: I do find that's true with how I react to stress. The way I used to react to stress before TM is very different from how I react to stress now.

BOB: More resilient.

JASPRE: I'm way more resilient.

BOB: You can look at TM simply: it gives the body a state of rest far deeper than the deepest part of beach sleep. It's very transformational in a real way, and it bubbles up and spills over to everything else in your life.

TM is a great tool.
Bob is an incredible gift.
x J

Wellness, Writing, and Self-Care

with Dr. Samantha Boardman

Positive Psychiatrist, and Author of Everyday Vitality

"Let's all focus more on each other."

SAMANTHA BOARDMAN, MD, *offers a unique perspective on the ever-sunny side of wellness. Dr. Boardman, a positive psychologist, believes that self-care and self-reflection are good, but too much of it can lead us down a harmful path. When this happens, we miss out on connections with others. I've always found Dr. Boardman's holistic approach, which focuses more on the expansive aspect of well-being, to be fascinating, refreshing, and inclusive.* **x Jaspre**

JASPRE: You have spoken quite a lot about how too much self-reflection can be detrimental. Why is this?

DR. SAMANTHA BOARDMAN: Self-reflection is important, and sometimes we don't have enough time to process things. We're all running on empty and not able to take a moment to pause and think, "Is that the way I wish I had responded? Is this the way I want to be living my life?" It's when self-reflection turns into rumination that it can take a darker turn. Rumination, when you're constantly mulling over your thoughts, is an on-ramp to depression. When you're so immersed in your thoughts and unable to lift yourself out, you can become unable to have perspective. You become entrenched and paralyzed.

Sometimes we co-ruminate with our best friends or loved ones. You know you're co-ruminating when it feels like Groundhog Day. You'll think, we've had this conversation before. We don't really feel better afterward. It's not this cathartic lift off your shoulders. If anything, co-ruminating embroils you in it again. Every time you retell that story, you're immersed in those same emotions that are kind of taking you on that downward spiral. We're not helping people when we're doing that, but it can almost masquerade as support.

JASPRE: How can we lift ourselves out of rumination?

SAMANTHA:

1. BEING IN NATURE and spending time outdoors.

2. COGNITIVE STRATEGIES OF SELF-DISTANCING, which is the opposite of self-immersion. Self-distancing would be thinking, "What would I tell a friend in this situation? What advice might I give them?"

3. OFFERING ADVICE IS ANOTHER SELF-DISTANCING STRATEGY. This comes from what is called Solomon's paradox. King Solomon was a very smart man who apparently would give great advice but was a total train wreck when it came to his own life. So when we lift out of ourselves and give advice, we are able to gain perspective. We suddenly have this clarity like, "Oh, my gosh, you should take that opportunity" or "You should think about doing this."

4. THINKING OF YOUR FUTURE SELF. Consider: Will this matter five years from now? Even three weeks from now?

5. ALSO, CONSIDER IF YOU WERE A FLY ON THE WALL. How would you describe this situation to somebody?

JASPRE: Are we treating anxiety the wrong way?

SAMANTHA: Anxiety really is discomfort. It's a feeling of powerlessness and uncertainty. There's a lot of messaging today that says, "You've got to be happy all the time and smiling all the time." There is so much perfectionism, especially in women. Everything has to be just right. We have an intolerance for discomfort. Our discomfort with discomfort is leading us astray. The result of that is avoidance. And we sort of green-lighted this idea that any challenge or anything that makes you feel uncomfortable is something to shield yourself from—but we end up building a wall around ourselves from anything uncomfortable. This leads to us disengaging and retreating from the world.

Avoidance in the moment can feel like a relief. I'll just stay home and watch this. I will disconnect. I can download this or go away. But this is all denial of how our well-being is deeply embedded in the connections we have, the communities that we exist in, and the world that we inhabit. It's so important to notice avoidance and to actually feel a little bit more comfortable around discomfort.

JASPRE: Is there merit to discomfort?

SAMANTHA: We feel more satisfied when we're doing things that stretch us. We tend to gravitate toward effort-sparing activities but it's actually when we are putting the effort in that we feel stronger. Even when it comes to writing letters—actually buying some stamps and getting some stationery. On Christmas, my mother used to always give me stationery in my stocking for me to write thank-you letters to people. I always thought it was cruel and unusual punishment. But she was on to something.

Apparently, one of the reasons we don't put things into writing is we feel like it's too awkward to thank someone for what they did for you. We feel it won't make a difference or we feel like it's going to make us look stupid. But we're actually depriving them of the opportunity to have a boost, and we're also depriving ourselves of the opportunity to give someone a boost like that. There are so many reasons that we hold ourselves back from communicating or connecting or doing things. It can be as simple as getting a pen and paper or even just writing something in bullet points. What do you admire about that person? What are you grateful for? Keeping that focus on someone else can remove that barrier.

JASPRE: How is letter-writing an important aspect of your practice and life?

SAMANTHA: I wrote a thank-you letter to my grandmother that my mother found after she died. My grandmother had written in the margins of it. Clearly, it meant something to her. And it meant so much to me that she had held on to it. It made me think of any time I've been reluctant to write somebody a note. Sometimes it'll just sit on my desk, or I won't do it. I try to remind myself of how it might mean something to somebody. I have a wall in my office that I think you have seen, it's full of letters that people have handwritten that mean the world to me. When I'm having a bad day, I just go over and look at them.

Finding letters that I've written to my kids or to my husband, there's so much to discover about where your head was at that moment. It doesn't have to be these deep major thoughts. There's so much pressure to be profound. Sometimes it's just the more mundane or the daily that gives us tremendous pleasure.

Writing can be really therapeutic. Just jotting down things that went well during the day can be meaningful. When we write, it helps us savor something. I'm a big believer in delight hunting. There's so much negativity in our everyday lives. Our brains are vigilant about what could possibly go wrong and that's what we hang on to. But when we are deliberate about delight, and when we're clocking things that are meaningful, and even writing it down in some way, it imprints on our brains differently.

Having positive prompts that can help us tap into our strengths helps us feel more powerful around what we value and what's meaningful to us.

DR. SAMANTHA BOARDMAN'S POSITIVE WRITING PROMPTS

Grab a pencil and paper and allow the following questions to guide you. Each one is meant to help you avoid unhealthy rumination and lean into positive self-reflection.

1. What are you looking forward to this week?
2. What are you going to do to make that happen?
3. What was a time when you were at your best? What strengths were you using during that time?
4. What is something you greatly value and hold dear? Why?

Dear Anyone on the Fence About Talking to a Therapist,

Therapy has helped me to connect the dots in my life. Talking to a therapist has benefits even when I'm in a good place in my life; it's incredible just to be able to share my thoughts with someone who will not judge. I've also learned from my therapist that it's okay to celebrate the good moments in life. It used to be that when I achieved something great, I'd just move on. But therapy has taught me to acknowledge the hard work I've done, and at least give myself a little pat on the back.

My generation has easier access to therapy, which is so necessary, particularly with all the time we spend online and the pressures of social media. Don't get me wrong, I think social media has benefits, but it can also be toxic. I'm guilty of feeling addicted to it at times, and it can be difficult to break the cycle. The toughest part for me when it comes to social media is the comparison aspect. I get so caught up wondering, "Why don't I look like that?" or "Why isn't my life as perfect as hers?" It's caused lots of anxiety in my life, but I'm trying to distance myself from it.

I know that I'm more than a picture. My generation needs to get off our phones, get out there, and enjoy nature! Enjoy life. I'm trying to do it every day, and I could always be better about it.

Life is heavy. There's so much pressure to do and say the right thing. Therapy can help you to recognize that social media does not reflect reality. The world of social media is so small compared to the bigger picture—the real world outside.

If you're ever struggling—with your self-image, your self-worth, with feelings of inadequacy, with social media, or just life in general—don't hesitate to seek out a therapist to talk to! There is absolutely no shame in asking for help.

Love, Maddie

Maddie Ziegler, actor and dancer

I am writing this for anyone living and suffering with depression and anxiety. I hope this helps you feel a little less alone and can offer some comfort that it will get better. You will get better.

I was nineteen when I was formally diagnosed with depression and anxiety after my housemate at uni found my detailed plan for ending my own life following a couple of years of feeling increasingly worthless, hopeless, and unlovable. When I told my parents that the doctor had prescribed medication and talking therapy, I was told that I just needed to try harder to be happy and that there was nothing wrong with me so I shouldn't be taking medication. So I didn't take the meds and I only attended two counseling sessions. Over the next ten years, I pitched and rolled through spells of moderate to severe depression and spells of feeling what I classed as "normal," feeling too scared to seek help for fear someone would tell me there was nothing wrong with me and that was just how everyone got through life. I developed severe social anxiety to the point I would shake, be physically sick, and feel like I couldn't breathe whenever I had to enter a new social situation. I spent two years unable to meet more than one friend at a time and never in a public place. I was regularly awake until 3 a.m. unable to stop thinking. I cried A LOT and was regularly having suicidal ideations and had a plan in place "just in case." When I was twenty-nine my (turns out pretty toxic) long-term relationship broke down and I started to rethink things. It was the kick up the ass that I needed to try and change things. I started with talking, really talking, to my best friend and sharing the dark in my head. She came with me to see a doctor who prescribed meds and CBT. This time I took the meds and saw out my prescribed CBT sessions. It has been a long road—my meds have been tweaked more times than I can remember, and CBT didn't work for me so I was referred to a wonderful psychologist who worked on Acceptance and Commitment Therapy with me, which gave me a solid platform that worked for me.

I'm now thirty-eight, and I have an amazing wife and beautiful two-year-old twin daughters. I still live with depression and anxiety. I will probably always need meds but that is okay. My last experience of suicidal thoughts and harmful behaviors was four years ago. I am now so much better than okay. I am now able to accept myself for who I am. I embrace my love of solitude rather than labeling myself "anti-social." My tendency to wear my emotions and sensitivity close to my skin, whilst sometimes feeling painful and anxiety-inducing, also allows me to feel empathy and compassion. I don't need a huge group of friends, and that doesn't mean I am unlikeable or unlovable. I can count my true friends on both hands and know that they have always got me and me them. My depression is and always will be a part of me, but it no longer defines me.

I am still here, and there have been many times where I did not expect to be. And for that, I am truly thankful. I hope if you have read this and feel like it resonates that you know that you are not alone. You are not the only one who feels like this.

" I am still here "

xo Sarah

...the act of trying to put words on them that made them seem true, made the writing come alive.

Exploring the Spiritual and Healing Aspect of Writing

with Dr. Mark Epstein

Psychotherapist and Author

"What our words on the page reveal to ourselves."

THERE'S A HEALING ASPECT OF WRITING, *which I and countless others know so well. Writing has helped me clarify my emotions, face my fears, and understand where I am and where I want to go. There's also a spiritual portal writing opens for us. It allows us to see our oneness. We're all so much more alike than different. Here, psychotherapist and author Mark Epstein, MD, tells us how writing has been a human practice and therapeutic tool for centuries. It is, as he says, purely "generous" to share our stories. In so many ways, writing has helped us evolve to where we are today.* **x Britt**

BRITT: **What role has writing played as a therapeutic tradition and tool?**

DR. MARK EPSTEIN: Writing has been a tradition for a long time in the psychoanalytic world—even going back to Freud, who wrote volumes and volumes, and lots of letters to figure himself out. *The Interpretation of Dreams,* which was journaling, was his beginning. His reflection on his history was the foundation of the whole psychoanalytic treatment.

I never thought of myself as a writer until I got married. My wife is an artist, and she was off, quickly after we moved in together, to her studio. And I was like, "What am I supposed to do while you're in the studio?" That's what got me started writing.

I found myself probing my own personal memories, both of being in therapy and of early experiences with Buddhism. And I found that by trying as hard as I could to accurately write those memories, as fleeting as they were, and sort of as small as they seemed—that the act of trying to put words on them that made them seem true, made the writing come alive.

BRITT: How has it helped you as a therapist?

MARK: Well, for example in my latest book, I decided I would try to capture in writing one psychotherapy session a week for a year. I went through and wrote a reflection on each session, trying to remember what might have been going on inside of me, and what I was thinking about. And then I showed everything that I had written to the various patients, so there was a back and forth about what I remembered happening in the session and then what I thought about what was happening. That whole experience proved very interesting. It shows how important writing has been and how helpful it can be.

BRITT: Can you offer an example?

MARK: I worked with a young woman whose mother had just died of ovarian cancer. She discovered in the aftermath of her mother's passing that she had the BRCA (breast cancer) gene. We had many conversations about it and, ultimately, she decided to have a double mastectomy.

She wrote an op-ed in the *New York Times*, and eventually a book, and I could see that writing about it helped her come to terms with this trauma.

I had another patient who lost her entire family in the Sri Lankan tsunami. She was the sole survivor. Years later we began working together. I encouraged her to start writing down some of what we talked about. That experience gave her a sort of second level of conversation about what we had already begun to process.

These writings became her book, *Wave*. She said in an interview in *The New Yorker* after the book came out that "Writing is a much better quality of agony than trying to forget."

BRITT: Do those who write about their experience gain so much from sharing their story because they've written it for both themselves and also for somebody else?

MARK: Well, you had the experience of writing your history up in a magazine, so you sort of know. It's both scary and courageous. And it's also very rewarding. What you inevitably find is that as unique as your personal experience is, the deeper commonality among all kinds of trauma is that everyone feels so alone in what happened to them.

The experience of being blindsided by life is going to happen to everyone at some time or another. Even if you make it through your whole life, you still die. So coming to terms with the fact that this happens, and then letting other people know through sharing your experience, is such a generous thing. And it always touches many more people than you could have ever expected. And that gives some value to what otherwise just feels like a terrible experience.

Are You Working on Your Shit?

When the great incredible dynamo that is Ms. Snow emailed
me asking for my thoughts on mental health I thought, "Holy
shit. On top of being a terrific person, a great actor, great
director, and great writer, Brittany is also tackling a huge
but neglected issue in most societies . . . mental health." (I'd
like to point out that if Brittany doesn't edit out the first
two sentences of this screed it will be a true miracle. Like
me, she hates compliments. Too bad for you, Brittany. Leave
it in!) Okay, mental health. Here's my intellectual and wise
perspective on the matter—as far as your brain and your soul
goes—in addition to a bunch of wonderful, cool, incredibly
good stuff in them . . . you have shit. I have shit. We all have
shit. No matter what. So get that shit talked out with a
professional at this shit. You go to a doctor for nonemergency
routine medical shit, right? So do the same for your mental
health. If you don't think you have shit, then you especially
need to go talk out your shit. This is coming from a guy
that knows he has shit but won't talk to a professional.
See? You thought I was working on my shit, right? Wrong. I'm
not. Not nearly like I should be. Negligible at best. Thank
God I have a wife who is extremely healthy when it comes to
dealing with one's shit because she's had a lot of shit, but I
know full well that her counsel is not enough. Why am I not
dealing with my shit? . . . Well, that's part of my shit. It's not
good. So . . . here's the deal . . . if you see me on the street . . .
you're free to ask me if I'm working on my shit. And if you
do this then I get to call you out on whether you're dealing
with your shit. Deal? Deal.

I wanted to !

This letter is the shit.

Joel McHale

Joel McHale, screenwriter, comedian, and actor

"Our stories are proof that we were here in this world — that we lived, loved, fought hard, and showed up every single day. Our stories become our legacies. It's important that we tell them."

— HANNAH BRENCHER

CHAPTER SIX

Friendship + Community

___

Dear twelve-year-old me,

I know you're struggling.

I know you feel like you are alone and lost in this big, confusing world right now.

You are trying so, so hard to understand how you ended up there. Living on the streets so young.

Trying to understand why your own mother would throw you out for loving someone, when she was supposed to love you no matter what.

Right now, you might feel like giving up.

Like there is no meaning for you to live.

Like all the bad things that happened to you living alone as a little girl on the streets are your fault.

But your eighteen-year-old self is here, writing you this letter and telling you to not give up.

The bad things are NOT your fault, and you will understand that when you are older.

The memories are still going to hurt, but you will not blame yourself anymore and you will be able to forgive those people for your own sake, so you will grow and heal.

You will find people who love you as their own child.

You will find a family where you belong and will be happy.

For many years, you're gonna be afraid to be yourself again. You will shut your friends and family out for a while because you are afraid of losing them the same way you lost your mother.

There will be hard times and many rock bottoms, but with the help of your new family and friends, you will get better.

You will get to the point where you are proud to be yourself once again.

This whole letter might be all over the place, but what I am trying to say here is, it will get better.

It's gonna take time and it will be a long, hard road, but you will be happy and loved again.

You will be happy to be alive again. You are strong.

You are loved.

And you are not alone.

The World Needs More Love Letters

with Hannah Brencher

Author and Founder of More Love Letters

WHEN HANNAH BRENCHER WAS TWENTY-TWO, *she moved to New York City filled with excitement for her new life. Soon after, she fell into a deep depression. To cope, she began writing letters to strangers and leaving them around the city. Putting ink to paper for those she didn't know helped her process her own feelings and to think of someone else during her loneliness, she tells us. Today, Hannah is the founder of The World Needs More Love Letters, a global organization that encourages the beautiful act of writing to those in need. She is also a writing instructor, the author of three books, and an advocate for encouraging a more inclusive conversation around mental health. We admire all that she does.* **xx Britt and Jaspre**

BRITT: How did starting your project, The World Needs More Love Letters, change your life? In what ways did this experience shape your perspective as a writer, educator, and mental health advocate?

HANNAH: I could never have imagined a movement growing out of such a small act but I am so thankful, every single day, that other people are impacted by this organization. Creating More Love Letters opened up the door for me to fulfill my biggest dream— becoming a writer. I never thought I would be a mental health advocate, but so many of the people we write to on a daily basis deal with depression and anxiety. I've found that my story can be a bridge to other people—a way to show someone it's okay to struggle and that there are people who want to surround you and support you and build you up with words of love.

This organization has made me more compassionate and empathetic as an educator, writer, and advocate for others.

JASPRE: When teaching writing, what do you most hope your students learn?

HANNAH: More than teaching people how to write well, my biggest lessons are in the art of discipline. We all have beautiful stories and experiences, but it takes showing up, day after day, to get those words down on the page. That's what makes the difference and that's what will truly form you as a writer if that is your goal. You must keep showing up. You must believe in yourself. You must believe that someone needs the stories you tell. If you can do that, it will change everything. It will add weight and power to the words you write.

BRITT: What do you see as the value of communicating our stories and our ideas through writing?

HANNAH: Sharing stories is a way for someone else to connect with us, nod their head, and maybe be able to say for the first time in their life, "Me too." That's powerful. I read the stories of others to feel known and to appreciate their life experiences. But I've also seen so many people experience freedom and joy and transformation because I wrote my stories down. Our stories are proof that we were here in this world—that we lived, loved, fought hard, and showed up every single day. Our stories become our legacies. It's important that we tell them.

> We all have beautiful stories and experiences, but it takes showing up, day after day, to get those words down on the page.

JASPRE: What is it about a handwritten letter that feels so magical to you?

HANNAH: Everything in the world is so digital these days. There's something beautiful about receiving a letter with someone's handwriting scrawled across the page. It's personal and it's something you can hold on to. I come across so many people who keep a box of letters from loved ones. In a world where everything is becoming paperless, people still want and need something to hold tight to. That's the power of writing a letter.

BRITT: How does writing a letter to a stranger differ from writing to someone you know?

HANNAH: I honestly prefer to write a letter to a stranger than to write one to someone I know. People always think it's brave to write to strangers, but you're kind of off the hook with strangers. You might never meet them. You can be brave enough to share your story with them. When you're writing to someone you know, more is at stake. It's personal. It's raw. You are baring your soul to someone you know. I think these letters are important to write, as hard as that task may be. You never know who in your life desperately needs to know they matter.

Storytelling Erases Invisibility

with Dr. Alfiee M. Breland-Noble, PhD

Psychologist, Scientist, and Founder of The AAKOMA Project

"Who we are, with all our uniqueness, is enough."

DR. ALFIEE M. BRELAND-NOBLE, PHD, *known as Dr. Alfiee, is a psychologist, scientist, and author. She is the founder of the AAKOMA Project, a thriving women of color–led mental health nonprofit that supports BIPOC and marginalized teens and young adults (and their families) as they manage their mental health through dialogue, equitable engagement in communities, and research. The root of Dr. Alfiee's work is authentic connection and ensuring every person—inclusive of all aspects of identity—receives the opportunity to achieve optimal mental health. "All too often, marginalized communities view mental health care as a privilege for the wealthy and feel unwelcome or disconnected from traditional providers," Dr. Alfiee, who is on the board of The Mental Health Coalition, tells us. "At the AAKOMA Project, we are working to change that perception."* **xx Jaspre and Britt**

JASPRE: How does storytelling play a role in facilitating better mental health?

DR. ALFIEE M. BRELAND-NOBLE: Storytelling is key, but it must be done in a way that allows both the storyteller and the listener to feel safe. This means being mindful of whose story we are sharing when we might inadvertently share things that will negatively impact other people and striking a healthy balance between sharing our story for healing vs. sharing it in a way that glorifies pain, suffering, and trauma.

BRITT: And writing specifically?

ALFIEE: Writing allows us to name, express, and often process our feelings concurrently. I find it to be a very useful tool.

I use writing to help me remember epiphanies and recall powerful experiences. Writing helps me put a stamp of approval and completion on my personal journey.

JASPRE: What is a key tool that you use for your own mental health?

ALFIEE: Exercise, mindfulness, and meditation are my go-to tools for my own mental health.

BRITT: What is one story of connection and storytelling that profoundly impacted your life?

ALFIEE: I was at a dinner with a group of incredibly bright, powerful, and accomplished women listening to stories of how we met the dinner honoree for the evening. The honoree then shared how she'd met each one of us and the impact we've had on her. When she got to me, she expressed two things that touched me deeply. First, she set the stage by describing that we'd met at a business gathering some years earlier where she and I were the only two Black women in the meeting. She said that she was blown away watching me use my brilliance and expert knowledge to overpower the people in that business meeting whom she knew had underestimated me and my intelligence. This comment made me cry.

It was one of the first times in my twenty-five-plus year career that someone ever referenced my knowledge and intelligence with respect to my craft. And here I was, three years after leaving academia, sitting at a dinner, with tears in my eyes because someone saw fully who I am—almost a quarter century into my career. It is so sad to think that so many marginalized people share this experience of being dismissed, disrespected, and devalued and here I was listening to someone tell me that she really saw me and respected me for my brains and skill.

What she did for me is what I strive to do every day in my work: encourage those of us from marginalized backgrounds to center our mental health and know that who we are, with all our uniqueness, is enough.

Writing helps me put a stamp of approval and completion on my personal journey

Dear September

Dear fourteen-year-old me,

Hi! To be honest, I've been really struggling to decide what to say to you. You've been through a lot recently, and you have a lot more coming your way. I promise, though, it gets better. You've moved out of the South and into a much more accepting community. You've gained some weight (and you've also gained some muscle). Every day you wake up surrounded by people you love and who love you. You have breakfast and coffee with your friends, and everything is good. You ran your first marathon in February, and you want to do another. You've discovered things you love to do. You make playlists that all your friends love. You sing and dance your heart out, even around other people. You have friends who support you. You are even able to talk about the boys and the girls you like with them. At almost twenty, you've still got a lot of growing to do. But you make efforts to improve every day. You still have bad days, but you know how to manage them. A few years from now, you find an article about Brittany Snow that you print out. You still keep it in your desk drawer as a reminder that things can get better. This letter will be joining it.

Love,
Grace-Anne

Sisters for Life

IN 2011, I WAS LUCKY ENOUGH TO DO A MOVIE *with a lot of singing, laughs, and badass women. Being a part of a cast that big, female, and filled with different personalities could have been tough but it was the exact opposite. The girls of* Pitch Perfect *formed a unique bond, which then solidified over the years into an unbreakable family. We've seen each other grow and change, fail and succeed. We've been through marriages, divorces, sicknesses, inside jokes, and tons of fun vacations. We've been there for each other in so many ways, as a symbol of strength and understanding. As sisters, lifelong friends, and a support system. Bellas for Life.* **xx Britt**

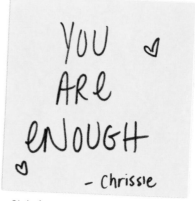

*Rebel
Wilson*

*Chrissie
Fit*

*Shelley
Regner*

*Chrissie
Fit*

HEALTH + WEALTH

Rebel Wilson

Fight to Keep on Keeping On!

Ester Dean

You are more loved than you would ever know

Anna Kendrick

I'm grateful for laughing + my health

Anna Camp

friends who Gets Me! BellasForLife

Ester Dean

I'm grateful for strong boss ladies to look up to & learn from. They inspire me ALWAYS!

Shelley Regner

I'm grateful for being AROUND LADIES who support + respect me ♡

Anna Camp

xo The Bellas

I don't think we give our friends enough credit.

And maybe it's not a universal thing, maybe it's a me thing. (That's what everybody thinks, right? Your problems are all on you?) Maybe, before now, I didn't put enough value into those close, irreplaceable bonds, and maybe it's a little late, but I'm learning just how incredibly important they are now.

I was stuck in a situation that caused me to be isolated from my friends for a long stretch of time, from the people who had been there throughout my whole life, to the point where I pretty much lost them all. It was dark and it was lonely, so much so that I clung onto the wrong people, whether in romantic relationships or otherwise, and that wasn't the right thing to do.

It's easy to get caught up with the wrong people, especially if you're easily led like I know I can be. And I hate the idea that anybody can relate to this, but I'm sure there are people who can. Please know that you're not alone, no matter how lonely things may feel.

After shedding those years of negativity, and the people who wanted to see me in that dark place, I have found my happiness with the right people, I have found light and positivity after that deep and lonely darkness. And if you have ever been in a similar situation, I believe that you can find strength in the right people, too.

Maybe it was just something nobody ever told me, that friendships are so, so important, but they are. And if you need a friend, I'm here.

Cherish your friends. And reach out, okay? Please, reach out. We're in this together, friend.

—Anonymous

Exploring Our Humanness through Letter-Writing

with Allyson Dinneen

Family therapist and the author of Notes from Your Therapist

"There's nothing wrong with hurting, grieving, or feeling sad."

SOCIAL MEDIA CAN BE A TRICKY PLACE SOMETIMES. *Connection feels hard to come by, and the pitfalls of comparison hard to avoid. But there is real wisdom to be found there, too, as evidenced by Allyson Dinneen's account @notesfromyourtherapist. On her Instagram account, Allyson shares heartfelt, honest, raw letters and words of encouragement with her many, many followers. "I love writing notes because it helps me capture for a moment the truth of my fleeting, changeable feelings and my reality," Allyson tells us. Somehow, her truths are always exactly what we need to read.* **xx Britt and Jaspre**

JASPRE: What do you love most about writing?

ALLYSON: I love to write because I've always needed to know what I'm feeling. I didn't have adults I could talk to as a kid and there were a lot of scary things going on around me. So I guess I learned to explore my inner world by writing down what was happening.

I love to talk, too, but writing is deeper sometimes than talking. For example, sometimes I don't know what it is I'm feeling. So I just write and mess around and I sort of stumble onto it. It helps too that handwriting is slower than talking. I'm interested in slowing down life however I can. The world rushes us in so many ways, and that's not so good for me.

BRITT: **What is the therapeutic value of short note-writing and affirmation-writing?**

ALLYSON: I prefer emotional reality and talking about what's already happening. Like when people express feeling hurt or confused. I feel like we're all less alone then. Especially if you didn't grow up that way. I always knew I was accepted if I was "happy" or without needs, but I wasn't at all sure I would be loved if I wasn't. I prefer the emotional truth of things as they are, probably because adults were so secretive when I grew up. No one talked about the big obvious things going on. It scared me that people pretended everything was fine. Even though I could feel so clearly that it wasn't.

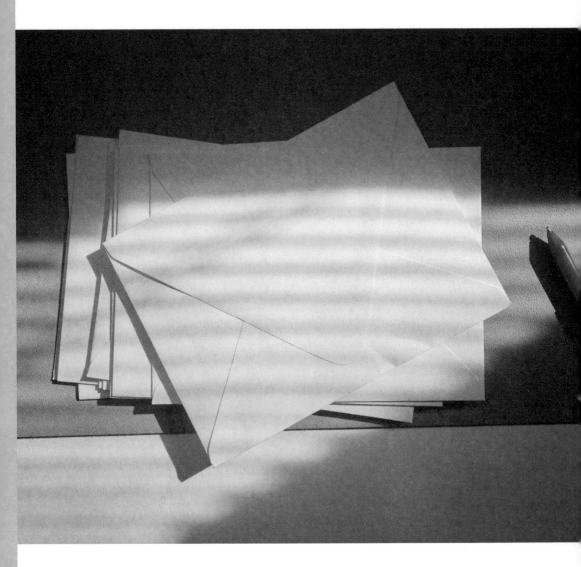

I'm definitely not a "try to think positive" person, and I think I'm negatively affected by a world that overvalues optimism and extraversion to such an extreme. I crave connection, vulnerability, and truth with people about pain and what hurts. I think other people do, too.

BRITT: What is a helpful tool for people when they are feeling down?

"Tune in to what you're actually feeling."

ALLYSON: To tune in to what you're actually feeling. Acknowledge the truth of it for a moment. We have to let go of the habit of avoiding and numbing ourselves to uncomfortable feelings, like we were taught to. It sounds strange but people often don't even know what they're feeling emotionally. They might have a general sense of being sad or angry, maybe, but that's about as far as they go with it because most of us have been taught to be ashamed of having feelings and that we should definitely try to avoid them.

The thing is: emotions are your body and your nervous system telling you how you're doing or what you need. You can't know what you need if you don't know how you feel. So it's pretty important information.

JASPRE: What has surprised you about how @notesfromyourtherapist has resonated so deeply with your community?

ALLYSON: I feel like people have a deep need to know or encounter things that are messy, imperfect, and vulnerable. Like we are.

Also I tend to write in the first person, and that might be a kind of indirect way of giving people a window to what I'm talking about: the universal nature of feelings and emotions. It seems like much of what people encounter from therapists who write is more instructive information. I really don't like telling others what to do. I'd rather just do my own thing and let other people figure out for themselves what they need.

I don't write as a therapist—I'm writing as a person who happens to be a therapist.

Human beings have brains that are highly evolved to learn from watching how other people do things. Not so much from being told what to do. So I guess I'm just letting people in.

I feel like people have a deep need to know or encounter things that are messy, imperfect, and vulnerable.

Exercises for a Happier Life

by Dr. Apostolos Lekkos

Functional and Energy Medicine Physician

> **WHEN I HAD A MYSTERY ILLNESS** *that no one could treat, two close friends connected me to Dr. Apostolos Lekkos. A former emergency room doctor, Dr. Lekkos left Western medicine more than a decade ago to open his functional medicine practice. His approach is riveting and accessible. For every patient he sees, he considers their mind, body, and spirit, often prescribing cathartic writing practices to help positively shift one's outlook on life. When Dr. Lekkos gave me "homework for my mind," I instantly wanted to share it with everyone.*
> **xxx Jaspre**

#1: PRE-SLEEP JOURNALING

Many patients I see have a difficult time sleeping. So I have them empty their mind by journaling their thoughts, worries, stresses, and feelings. The subconscious mind is extremely active when we sleep and holds all our life stressors. This is a big reason why many of us have sleep difficulties. Putting our worries on paper can help purge these issues, thus clearing the mind for better, more restful sleep.

#2: HIGH-VIBRATION WRITING

This exercise focuses on turning a pessimist into an optimist. It is also done before bed, so we plant seeds into the subconscious mind.

Studies show that pessimists have more medical illnesses than the general population and they die earlier. Optimists live an average of seven and a half years longer. Fortunately, mindset is believed to be only 25 percent hereditary, meaning we have some control over our outlook via positive thoughts.

Our thoughts have energy. Our thoughts have power. Our thoughts can change the vibration of our cells. Negative thoughts have a slower vibration, which is more consistent with illness while positive thoughts have a higher vibration and create a healthier state of being. People with constant negative thoughts remain in a lower vibrational state, which can promote a higher chance of a disease process.

To change someone's attitude around their life, I have them journal three good things that happened to them that day, not what they're grateful for. These must be actual good things that happened or that were perceived to be good. As you do this exercise, you cannot repeat anything you've already written down. It's one and done.

After a few days, you will get stuck because you've used up all the obvious good things in your life. This forces you to really think about your day, which causes you to look at the small, happy things: that first aromatic sip of coffee in the morning; the sun warming your face when you go check the mailbox; the laughter of your children in the living room as you cook dinner.

When you write these things down right before bed, you start training the subconscious to look for the good things in the everyday. After a while, you'll notice your days becoming more positive, and life becoming richer and more exciting. Overall, you'll feel happier. Your subconscious is finding the good things without you even noticing. What you will notice is food tasting better, people being more pleasant, the work commute being far more enjoyable. Your life will generally seem more positive. Through that lens, you'll be able to really see the wonders of life and truly enjoy them . . . for seven and a half years longer!

Caring for Our Bodies and Rewriting Our Stories

I love you kim! ♡ B **with Kim Shapira**

Dietician and Nutrition Therapist

"You can be anything you want to be in this moment."

KIM SHAPIRA'S WORK *as a nutrition therapist has helped countless people shift how they relate to food, emotional eating, and their bodies. She is a dietician revolutionary who has helped me and many others see triggers and let go of expectations. And she incorporates letter-writing into her practice in a way that is so visceral and beautiful. I learned from Kim to take better care of my body. I've also learned that life doesn't have to be perfect. Life doesn't have to be linear, either. What's important, as Kim reveals here, is that we learn to live day by day, moment by moment. We need to allow ourselves to take a pause, remove ourselves from triggers, shed labels, and stay in the now.* **xx Britt**

BRITT: You help people reframe their relationship to eating and their bodies. Take us back to what prompted this work.

KIM: When I was twelve, I got sick. I had to have lots of reconstructive surgeries and see many specialists. There were classes taught about my problem. My body was studied. It was traumatizing. Whenever I went to the doctor—and there were always long waits for different specialists—my mom would say, "Don't cry. Let me take you shopping." I would dream of what I was going to buy after my appointment. This cemented in me a very powerful shopping addiction. So from there, anytime I went through something triggering or traumatizing, my mind immediately thought of Nordstrom.

When I got much older, I started to understand that trigger and connection. I knew I wanted to be in a career where I can help people get healthy.

But my client work was more nuanced than I was prepared for. My solutions didn't always work in a way that I could predict. I needed to learn more. So I went on to study spiritual psychology, neuropsychology, quantum physics, and all the different modalities that people use to heal themselves. In the process, I started to understand that my shopping is very much like people's eating. The more I understood the way our minds worked, the more I kind of homed in on removing restrictions and diets. I started concentrating on not what somebody is eating but on why they were eating. I created this method based on the idea of sustainable health and weight loss. And that's where I've had success.

BRITT: How has letter-writing helped you in your journey?

KIM: Letter-writing has been about going back and understanding—with complete gratitude—that I could not do what I'm doing and help so many people if I had not overcome this myself. Letter-writing has helped me be in touch with my inner child and the impact it has had on who I am as an adult.

That's one of the most gratifying things: knowing that your story matters to somebody else and that you didn't go through what you went through for no reason.

BRITT: If you could write a letter to your body, what would you say?

KIM: I'm someone who believes that my body is separate from who I am. I have so much appreciation for the way that my body shows up for me. Every single day. I have so much gratitude for it. So I would say: thank you. I will honor you every chance that I get. And I will see you, I will recognize the signs, and I will take great care of you.

BRITT: We tend to forget that we have this body that houses our soul and that we need to take care of it. Yet, we'll feed it cookies and hope for the best. I need to remind myself that I need to be nice to my body because it's gotten me this far.

KIM: Yes!

BRITT: I'll often forget that I'm feeding my mind and not my body. This happens when I'm triggered. How do you talk about this in your work?

KIM: I spend many hours of the day helping people create that reflex of finding their mind. Our minds often escape our bodies. I want people to recognize that they need to bring their mind back to their body so then they can scan it.

Think of this: People have very healthy relationships with their bladder, for the most part. When their bladder tells them it must go to the bathroom, they think, I see you. I know I can hold it for a bit, but I will take care of you. But people forget to take care of their stomach and what it's telling them. That is mostly because their mind is not in their body. They're eating because they've been triggered, and when somebody's triggered they stop moving forward.

BRITT: You talk a lot about how we are really a soul housed in a body. How do we best feed our soul while taking care of our body?

KIM: The work that needs to be done is to recognize ego thoughts vs. soul thoughts. Ego thoughts are labels that we attach ourselves to. They're what we think we have to show up as. But we need to recognize that we don't have to please anyone. We have to be good people and open-hearted. But we don't have to give all our energy to people, we don't have to let them take it. To be soul-based—to be nourishing to your soul—is to recognize that I can be anything I need to be at this moment. I don't have to be full of labels. I can be anything. And then it's important to find people that will allow you to grow and change, so you can continue to be anything at this moment.

BRITT: Our stories and labels can be so ingrained in our brain. How do we rewrite them?

KIM: There are two parts. First, you see the story. If you can see the challenge, you can see the temptation. It cannot affect you. Learning how to remain unaffected by things is the goal. Remember, you can't stop the thoughts. We have sixty thousand thoughts in response to whatever we see, smell, feel, or hear. But we can work on the way we react. It's about working on the space between the thought and the action.

The second part is to write a letter. Write with such gratitude and appreciation. Shine a new light. For me, I can look back at my doctors, who I have a visceral hatred for. I can then put myself in my twelve-year-old body and I look at them, each one of them, and see them: I can see that they just wanted to help me. I can put my gratitude for them in my letter.

Once you've done that, sign the letter with love.

Burn it.

And bury it.

Why We Need
to Journal
to Ourselves

with Carolyn Costin MA, MEd., MFT

....

Eating Disorder Therapist, Author

"Give all parts of you a voice."

CAROLYN COSTIN *is a renowned clinician and author who treats people struggling with eating disorders and trains clinicians and coaches. Her perspective is unique, as she was the pioneer in writing openly about her eating disorder and her recovery. She's lived it. She's overcome it. And today, she combines her personal experience, evidence-based treatment, and Eastern healing modalities with writing practices to provide a profoundly healing philosophy for those struggling. By sharing her story, Carolyn has helped so many heal.* **x Britt**

BRITT: **What made you want to first share about your eating disorder publicly?**

CAROLYN: When I started writing about my eating disorder, I wasn't sure who would be affected by my story. I first wrote about it for a local newspaper, over forty years ago now, and the people came out of the woodwork after reading that article.

I always wanted to share that you can recover. People were being treated at that point in a twelve-step program for addiction, where you'd always be recovering. But I was recovered. It was over. I wanted to get that out there.

During my recovery, I kept a journal. Now in my practice as a therapist, I teach people to journal. Among other things, I guide them to write letters to themselves and to write down traumatic events that they cannot talk about. Fifteen years into my practice, I sent out a survey to all the patients that I had treated. Somewhere between eighty-five and ninety percent of the people who were recovered all did three things—they stopped weighing, they reached out for help when struggling, and they journaled. I find that fascinating.

BRITT: Why is writing so helpful to people? Is it the release of emotions? Or just the self-care found in taking time for yourself to write?

CAROLYN: It's both. There are neurological aspects to it. We use a different part of our brain when we write. When you focus on a problem, you can get stuck in your mind in this feedback loop. What I find people do is jump ahead of themselves.

One of the main ways people heal through writing is what I call strengthening your healthy self. Let's say someone has a binge-eating disorder and they have a hard time stopping when they want to binge. I'll tell them to write down all the reasons why they want to do it. Then I'll ask them to write back from the part of themselves that wants to stop, their "healthy self" or the part that's coming to see me for help.

If you end up binging, it's okay in the beginning. Stopping a habitual behavior is a process. It's not about telling yourself, "I'm going to write instead of binging." That won't work. Instead, I want to give voice to the part of you that would like to stop this behavior. That's strengthening your healthy self.

BRITT: I would love to think that I can say, "I'm going to take care of myself," right at that moment.

CAROLYN: What you must do is say, "I want access to the part of me that wants to take care of me and to stop binging, because somehow when I feel like binging that part of me is not there." People need to write a dialogue from the part of them that wants to binge, which is their eating disorder self, and the part that wants to stop, which is their healthy self.

When they come to my office, the client will say, "I want to stop binging," but then they continue to do it anyway. I tell them that they need to journal the thoughts from the part that wants to binge, the part that says things like, "I'm sick of people telling me what to do, I don't care if I gain weight." I tell them to let it all come out because that needs to be expressed. Then I teach them to write back from their healthy self. When they feel stuck, I ask what they would say to someone else in their situation. They always know how they would help someone else, so this is about getting them to apply that to themselves.

Even if they can't write from the healthy self at that moment, I'll have clients bring this writing to me, and I will give it back to them and say, "Okay, the battle is between you and you." So how do we access those two parts? Journaling is the closest way I've found. Writing is a way of expressing, of getting it out there, getting the two different parts of self in a dialogue and it helps calm the emotional aspect.

I've done this & it was very helpful and pretty cool ✶

In her practice, Carolyn Costin encourages clients to write letters to themselves. She holds on to the letters and mails them back to the person in six months to a year. The practice opens a new lens through which you can see yourself—from your fears to your hopes to your growth. "It's fascinating when you get it back," she says.

HERE'S CAROLYN'S PROMPT: Gather a small group of friends. Each of you pen a letter to yourself and give it to someone in the group to keep. Have that person mail your letter to you in a year. You do the same for someone else in the group.

Reflect on where you were then and where you are now.

Just remember that you are not alone. There are several people out there who are willing to help you heal and who want to be there for you every step of the way.

....

....

....

....

....

....

....

....

....

....

....

....

....

....

....

RIGHT NOW.

This moment.

Pick up a pencil.

Tear off a piece of paper.

And write a letter to someone.

Someone from long ago.
Someone from the future.
Someone from your heart.
Someone from your mind.

Write what you feel.

Don't hold back.

Let yourself go.

Write for them.

Write through it.

WRITE FOR YOU.

Resources

Sometimes we need more support than writing and reading letters. We all experience hard times. Know that you are not alone. If you or someone you know is struggling, there are many forms of support. Please see below.

NATIONAL SUICIDE PREVENTION LIFELINE: 988

If you or someone you know is in crisis, whether they are considering suicide or not, please call the toll-free lifeline to speak with a trained crisis counselor 24/7. suicidepreventionlifeline.org or 988lifeline.org

NATIONAL SEXUAL ASSAULT HOTLINE: 1-800-656-HOPE

Connect with a trained staff member from a sexual assault service provider in your area that offers access to a range of free services. Free help, 24/7. rainn.org

VETERANS CRISIS LINE: 1-800-273-8255 or text 838255, or dial 988 and press 1.

If you're a veteran in crisis or concerned about one, there are caring, qualified VA responders standing by to help 24/7. The Veterans Crisis Line is a free, anonymous, confidential resource that's available to anyone, even if you're not registered with VA or enrolled in VA health care. veteranscrisisline.net

CHILD ABUSE (CHILDHELP): 1-800-4-A-CHILD

Provides 24/7 assistance in 170 languages to adults, children, and youth with information and questions regarding child abuse. All calls are anonymous and confidential.

CRISIS TEXT LINE: Text HOME to 741741

Connect with a trained crisis counselor to receive free, 24/7 crisis support via text message. crisistextline.org

NATIONAL DOMESTIC VIOLENCE HOTLINE: 1-800-799-SAFE, or text START to 88788

Trained expert advocates are available 24/7 to provide confidential support to anyone experiencing domestic violence or seeking resources and information.

THE TREVOR PROJECT LIFELINE (LGBTQ): 1-866-488-7386

This lifeline receives over 45,000 calls each year assisting LGBTQ youth. Call if you are a young person in crisis, feeling suicidal, or in need of a safe and judgment-free place to talk. thetrevorproject.org

NATIONAL PARENT HELPLINE: 1-855-4-A-PARENT

Helpline for parent and caregiver support.

NATIONAL HUMAN TRAFFICKING HOTLINE: 1-888-373-7888

National and confidential toll-free hotline to report trafficking or connect with anti-trafficking services, 24/7, available in 200 languages. Text also available for survivors: text HELP to BEFREE (233733) from 3 p.m. to 11 p.m.

September Letters is proud to partner with The Mental Health Coalition as we work together to end the stigma surrounding mental health.

The Mental Health Coalition provides access to mental health resources via their library at thementalhealthcoalition.org. You can browse this database to learn about mental health, help a loved one, learn coping skills, and seek support.

We all have mental health, and it's more important now than ever that we take care of ourselves.

Acknowledgments

Dear September,

WE WANT TO THANK YOU, our September Letters community, who has shown up more passionately and clearer than we ever could have imagined. It is because of you and your letters that you are holding this book! We are in awe of the strength and courage in sharing your stories. Know that you have helped someone feel less alone and more connected. That is the greatest gift; we are so grateful to you.

TO EVERY SINGLE EXPERT WE SPOKE WITH, thank you for taking time out of your busy schedule. It was an honor and a privilege to spend time with you and listen to your story: Jay Shetty, #1 *New York Times* bestselling author, purpose coach, former monk, host of the number-one health and wellness podcast *On Purpose*, and chief purpose officer of Calm; Kim Shapira, MS, RD; Allyson Dinneen, M.Ed., MFT; Diana Chao, founder and executive director at Letters to Strangers; Pooja Lakshmin, MD; Hannah Brencher, author and founder of More Love Letters; Mark Epstein, MD; Dr. Wendy Suzuki, professor of neural science and psychology and dean of the College of Arts and Science at New York University; Carolyn Costin, MA, MEd., MFT; Ana Tucker, Board Certified Hypnotherapist, Master Neurolinguistic Programming (NLP) Practitioner, and a Licensed Clinical Social Worker; David Kessler, author, public speaker, and grief expert; Dr. Alfiee Breland-Noble, psychologist, scientist, mental health correspondent, and founder of the AAKOMA Project; Jodi Ann Bickley, founder of One Million Lovely Letters; Naomi Torres-Mackie, PhD, licensed clinical psychologist, and head of research at the Mental Health Coalition; Geneen Roth, author and teacher; Gretchen Rubin, author; Grace Harry, Joy Strategist; Bob Roth, CEO, David Lynch Foundation; Beth Hutchens, cofounder and creative director of Foundrae; Samanthan Boardman, MD; Alex Elle, author and restorative writing teacher; Anna Quindlen, novelist and journalist; Jason B. Rosenthal, public speaker and author of *My Wife Said You May Want to Marry Me*; and Dr. Apostolos Lekkos, functional and energy medicine physician.

TO OUR FRIENDS: Hannah Bronfman, Dewanda Wise, Torrey Devitto, Anna Camp, Jennifer Kaytin Robinson, Joel McHale, Kelley Jakle, Chrissie Fit, Lily Cornell Silver, Amanda Kloots, Andrew Gelwicks, Rebel Wilson, Ester Dean, Shelly Regner, Anna Kendrick, Jordana Brewster, Sam Richardson, Santiago Cabrera, Maddie Ziegler, Hayley Kiyoko, Maria Menounos, Harrison Miller, Scott Mescudi, and Tom Hanks. Thank you for taking the time to write letters and share your stories. To Liz Sullivan, Jessica Sindler, and Emily Hillebrand, thank you for helping us workshop in the early days.

To Meg Thompson, our literary agent and sister, thank you for believing in us before we believed in ourselves and for making this process so magical. We have nothing but immense love for you.

To Stacey Lindsey, our September Letters editorial director and creative collaborator, thank you for understanding our vision. Your deep care, understanding, and warmth is felt and seen.

To our entire Harper Design team, especially Sarah Haugen, our editor, thank you for shepherding us with such care; Lynne Yeamans and Raphael Geroni, thank you for bringing our vision to beautiful vivid life; Stacey Fischkelta and Dori Carlson, thank you for keeping us on track; Leslie Cohen and Katie O'Callaghan for amplifying our message; and finally to Marta Schooler and Jonathan Burnham: We are so honored to be published by you. Thank you for believing in this book's mission, and for all of your savvy guidance and support.

To our family at the Mental Health Coalition: Kenneth Cole, founder and chairman of the board, thank you for helping to end the stigma around mental health. We are in awe of you. Jennifer Moore, executive director, thank you for instantly making us feel like part of the family. Catie Cole, cofounder, thank you for consistently spreading the word and supporting our mission. Nicole Moriarty, senior director of Programs and Partnerships, thank you for always being a guiding light.

To our September Letters team: Thank you to Tatum of Brandt Creative for running our digital; to Natalie for making sure we never lost anything and for picking up the pieces; Rachel Joanis for bringing our babies to life, Lauren Withrow for capturing all of our gorgeous lifestyle photos, Alec Kugler for always being there for us by capturing our true selves, Tereza for being our Pinterest Queen, Meagan for amplifying our message, Heather for your all-encompassing protection, Natalie and Sam for your support, and to Kristina for keeping watch. Thank you to Liz Malone for being our guardian angel.

To Billie and Papaya, our furry angels who watch over us, we love you forever. Thank you for always being in our lives.

xxx

Bill + Jaspre

About the Authors

Activist and actress Brittany Snow has been championing conversations around mental health for more than fifteen years. She is a passionate and outspoken advocate for mental health awareness and well-being. She is the cofounder of the nonprofit movement Love is Louder with the Jed Foundation and MTV. In 2020 she started the letter-writing and therapeutic experience September Letters with friend Jaspre Guest. She has written, directed, and produced a movie about mental health and addiction that will be released in 2023. She is a metaphysics and science fiction fan and loves escape rooms, puzzles, and mysteries. She hopes one day to have ten more rescue dogs because Billie and Charlie are her favorite things.

Creative entrepreneur and activist Jaspre Guest created her career by shunning traditional norms. Known as the fixer, she is the founder of boutique branding and public relations agency Noise 784. Jaspre has led initiatives for a range of nonprofits including It Gets Better, Global Citizen, the International Rescue Committee, Love Is Louder, and the ASPCA. In 2020, she cofounded the letter-writing initiative September Letters with friend Brittany Snow. Jaspre's next project, Finding Your Magic, will fulfill her desire to help people by creating a hub for metaphysical healing. She has been featured in *People*, E!, *Forbes*, and Coveteur. Jaspre is obsessed with her fruit salad, aka her Pomeranians: Papaya, Fig, Rhubarb, and Quince.

Inspired by the full-circle moment
in the coffee shop, here is your own
back pocket to keep your letter! ——————▶

We hope this book has inspired you to
write your truth for yourself or for
someone else who needs it.

Our website is available for more ideas
and organizations who would love your
story of hope. Thank you for being a part of
    our community. ♥ D + J